Shortcuts to Success

Maths

Junior Certificate
Ordinary Level

Marc Halpin

GILL & MACMILLAN

Gill & Macmillan Ltd
Hume Avenue
Park West
Dublin 12
with associated companies throughout the world
www.gillmacmillan.ie

© Mark Halpin 2006
ISBN-13: 978 07171 3918 7
ISBN-10: 0 7171 3918 2

The paper used in this book is made from the wood pulp of managed forests. For every tree felled, at least one tree is planted, thereby renewing natural resources.

Contents

Preface

This maths revision book was written to help you, the student, revise all areas of the Junior Certificate Ordinary Level maths course, thereby achieving your potential in the Junior Certificate Examination.

The Ordinary Level maths course is quite a long and detailed one. This revision book, however, breaks the course into twelve topics and covers each one in detail. The style used is very student-friendly with areas of importance highlighted and diagrams used throughout.

The revision book features the following:

* **A unique layout**

The Junior Certificate examination consists of two papers with six topics on each. This revision book has a similar format. Also, I have attempted to group the topics as they may appear in the examination.

* **Comprehensive revision of the entire course**

Each topic is explained thoroughly with excellent examples and solutions given on all parts.

* **Detailed questions and solutions**

At the end of each chapter, a number of exam type questions are asked based on the revised material. These questions are exam standard.
The solutions are carefully worked through to enable the student to see where s/he may have gone wrong and also to see the correct layout for such questions.

* **Sample papers and solutions**

The revision book also contains sample papers (with unique questions) with detailed, worked-through solutions.

This revision book is an excellent tool with which to prepare yourself for the forthcoming Junior Certificate exam. Please remember though: 'The most important maths revision is the doing, not the reading'. If you revise and complete the questions inside as well as you can, I am sure that you will find each topic is much more manageable.

I wish all students sitting the Junior Certificate examination in June great success. I hope you find this book beneficial as you prepare for the mathematics exam.

Marc Halpin
Coláiste Choilm
Ballincollig
Co. Cork

Chapter 1
Sets

Section A
2-Set Venn Diagram

It is very important that we know the different areas of a Venn diagram involving 2 sets.

① Union and intersection

(i) $\underline{A \cup B}$ (*A union B*)

All of set *A* as well as all of set *B*.

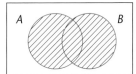

(ii) $\underline{A \cap B}$ (*A intersection B*)

The area which is in both sets.

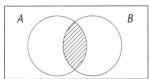

② Compliment

(i) $\underline{A'}$ (*A compliment*)

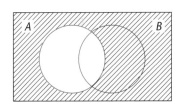

Everything outside set *A*.

(ii) $\underline{(A \cup B)'}$ (*A union B compliment*)

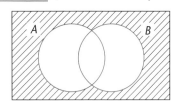

Everything outside *A* union *B*.

③ Less

(i) $\underline{A/B}$ (*A less B*)

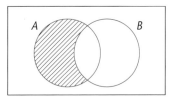

The area in set *A* which isn't in set *B*.

(ii) $\underline{B/A}$ (*B less A*)

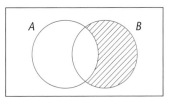

The area in set *B* which isn't in set *A*.

Summary of the various areas

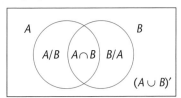

Section B
How to Fill Out a Venn Diagram

Example 1

Given $U = \{1, 2, 3, 4, 5, 6, 7\}$
         $P = \{1, 2, 3, 4\}$
         $R = \{3, 6, 7\}$

Complete the Venn diagram below:

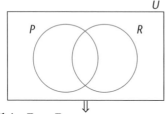

① *Fill in* $P \cap R$.
(the element(s) in both sets)

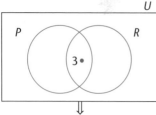

② Fill in the remaining elements of P and R.

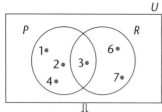

③ Fill in the elements in U but not in P or R.

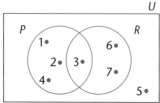

Example 2

Given $U = \{a, b, c, d, e, f, g, h\}$
         $M = \{b, d, f, h\}$
         $N = \{d, g, c\}$

Complete the Venn diagram below:

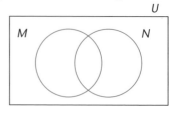

Hence list the elements of:

(i) M/N
(ii) M'
(iii) $M \cap N$
(iv) $(M \cup N)'$
(v)   Find # N'
(vi) Find # $(M \cap N)'$

Solution

① $M \cap N$

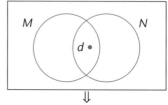

②   The remainder of both sets.

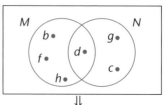

③   In U but not in M or N.

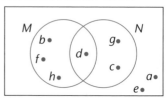

(i) _M/N_

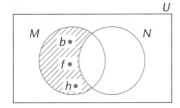

$= \{b, d, f, h\} / \{d, g, c\}$

$= \{b, f, h\}$

(ii) _M′_

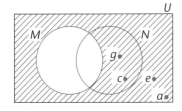

All elements outside _M_.

$= \{e, a, g, c\}$

(iii) _M ∩ N_

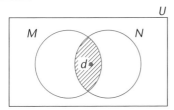

The elements common to both sets.

$= \{d\}$

(iv) _(M ∪ N)′_

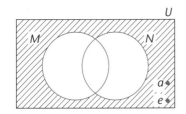

The elements in _U_ but not in _M_ or _N_.

$= \{e, a\}$

(v) **Find # _N′_**

> # [cardinal number] means _'how many elements are there'_

$N' = \{b, f, h, a, e\}$

$\Rightarrow \# N' = 5$

> **Please notice that the answer to a question involving a cardinal number is never in a bracket.**

(vi) **Find # _(M ∩ N)′_**

$(M \cap N)' = \{b, f, h, g, c, a, e\}$

$\Rightarrow \# (M \cap N)' = 7$

Section C
Written Problems

There are two types of written problems which may be asked involving 2-set Venn diagrams. They are very popular and must be known.

Type 1

There are 30 pupils in a class. Each pupil is asked to name their favourite soccer player. 16 said Damien Duff and 12 said Robbie Keane while 5 liked both players. Illustrate the information on a Venn diagram and hence find:

(i) How many like neither player.

(ii) How many like Damien Duff only.

① **Fill in those who like *both*.**

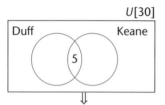

② **Complete both sets.**

$$\begin{bmatrix} 16 - 5 = 11 \\ 12 - 5 = 7 \end{bmatrix}$$

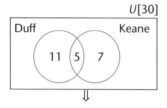

③ **Fill in those *outside* the sets.**

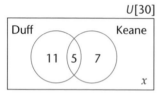

We are not told how many like neither, so let this be x.

Solve for x

$$11 + 5 + 7 + x = 30$$
$$23 + x = 30$$
$$x = 30 - 23$$
$$\Rightarrow \qquad \underline{x = 7}$$

(i) Therefore 7 pupils like neither player.

(ii) From the diagram, we see that 11 pupils like Damien Duff only.

Type 2

20 people were asked whether they prefer tea or coffee. 13 prefer tea, 8 prefer coffee while 2 don't like either drink. Illustrate the information above on a Venn diagram and hence find:

(i) How many like both tea and coffee.

(ii) How many like coffee but not tea.

① Fill in how many liked *both* drinks.

(Because we are not told how many like both, let the intersection of the sets be x)

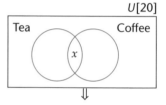

② Complete the sets.

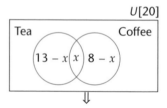

③ Fill in those who like neither.

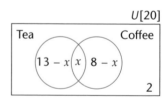

Solve for x

$$(13 - x) + x + (8 - x) + 2 = 20$$
$$13 - x + x + 8 - x + 2 = 20$$
$$\Rightarrow \qquad 13 + 8 - x + 2 = 20$$
$$23 - x = 20$$
$$-x = 20 - 23$$
$$-x = -3$$
$$\Rightarrow \qquad \underline{x = 3}$$

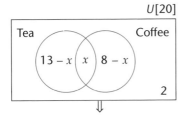

Fill in for $x = 3$

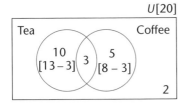

(i) Therefore 3 liked both drinks.

(ii) 5 people liked coffee but not tea.

Section D
Subsets and Equal Sets

Note 1   *Subsets [⊂]*

① Set A is a subset of set B if all elements in A are also in B.

② Every set is a subset of itself.

③ The null set is a subset of every set.

⇩

Write down the subsets of $X = \{2, 3, 4\}$.
$\{2\}$ $\{3\}$ $\{4\}$ $\{2, 4\}$ $\{2, 3\}$ $\{3, 4\}$ $\{\ \}$ $\{2, 3, 4\}$
                                  ↑   ↑
                              Null   The set
                              set   itself

Note 2   *Equal sets (=)*
Two sets are equal if they contain exactly the same elements.

⇩

Given $M = \{c, d, e\}$ and $N = \{e, c, d\}$ we say $M = N$ as they contain the same elements.

Example

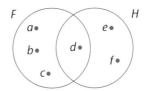

Insert the relevant symbol(s)
⊂, ⊄, =, ≠, ∈, ∉ in each of the following statements:

(i) $\{a\} \ldots F$

(ii) $a \ldots F$

(iii) $\{d, e, f\} \ldots H$

(iv) $b \ldots F$

(i) $\{a\} \ldots F$

Because a is inside two brackets, $\{a\}$ is a *set* and *not* an element.

⇒ $\{a\} \subseteq F$ and $\{a\} \neq F$

(ii) $a \ldots F$

'a' is not in brackets so it is the *element a*.

⇒ $a \in F$

(iii) $\{d, e, f\} \ldots H$

$\{d, e, f\}$ contains the same elements as set H.

⇒ $\{d, e, f\} = H$

and $\{d, e, f\} \subseteq H$

(iv) $b \ldots F$

Again, b is an element and not a set.

$\Rightarrow \quad b \underset{\ddot{\cdot}}{\in} F$

Again, it is vey important that the areas of a Venn diagram involving 3 sets are known.

---

① Union and intersection

(i) $C \cup D$

All of set C as well as set D.

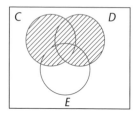

(ii) $C \cup D \cup E$

All of set C and all of set D and all of set E.

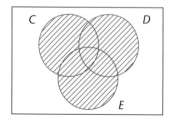

(iii) $C \cap E$

The area in C and also in E.

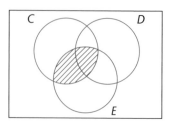

(iv) $C \cap D \cap E$

The area in all three sets.

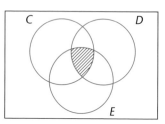

---

② Compliment

(i) $(C \cup D)'$

Everything outside set C and set D.

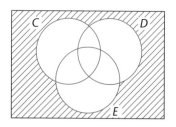

(ii) $(C \cup D \cup E)'$

Everything outside set C, set D and set E.

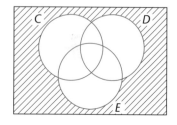

6

③ Less

(i) $(C \cup D)/E$

- Look at all of set C and set D.
- Take set E away from it.

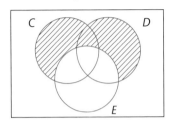

(ii) $E/(C \cup D)$

- Look at set E.
- Take all of set C and set D away.

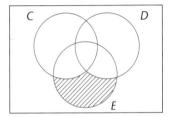

Summary of the various areas

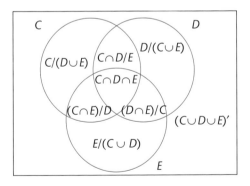

Section F
How to Fill Out a Venn Diagram

Given $U = \{a, b, c, d, e, f, g, h\}$

$R = \{a, c, d, f\}$

$S = \{c, e, b\}$

$T = \{c, a, e, g\}$

complete the Venn diagram.

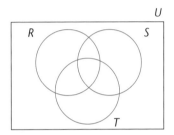

Complete the Venn diagram *from the middle out* as shown below:

①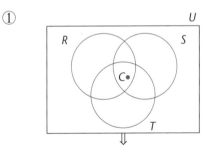

c is in all three sets

②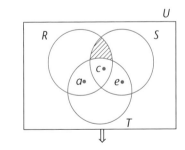

- $R \cap T = \{a, c\}$
- $R \cap S = \{c\}$ only
- $S \cap T = \{c, e\}$

③

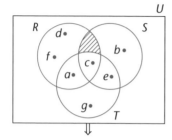

- $R = \{a, c, d, f\}$
- $S = \{c, e, b\}$
- $T = \{c, a, e, g\}$

④

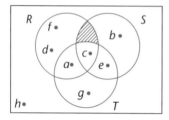

- $\{h\}$ is in U but not in sets R, S or T.

Example

Given the diagram below, find the elements of:

(i) $A \cup B$

(ii) $B/(A \cup C)$

(iii) $(B \cup C)/A$

(iv) $A \cap B \cap C$

(v) $(A \cup C)'$

(vi) Find # $(A \cup B)/C$

(vii) Find # $(A \cup B \cup C)'$

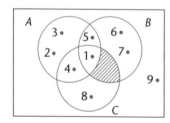

(i) $\underline{A \cup B}$

All the elements in set A as well as those in set B

$= \{3, 2, 4, 1, 5, 6, 7\}$

8

(ii) $\underline{B/(A \cup C)}$

① Look at set B in the diagram.

② Take away everything in $A \cup C$.

③ What are you left with?

$\Rightarrow$ $\{\underline{1}, \underline{5}, 6, 7\}/\{1, 2, 3, 4, 5, 8\}$

$= \{6, 7\}$

> **It is advisable to do the question in this way to pick up the maximum *attempt* marks.**

(iii) $\underline{(B \cup C)/A}$

$= \{\underline{4}, \underline{1}, \underline{5}, 6, 7, 8\}/\{1, 2, 3, 4, 5\}$

$= \{6, 7, 8\}$

(iv) $\underline{A \cap B \cap C}$

The element(s) in all three sets

$= \{1\}$

(v) $\underline{(A \cup C)'}$

Everything outside $A \cup C$

$= \{6, 7, 9\}$

(vi) $\underline{\text{Find # } (A \cup B)/C}$

$(A \cup B)/C$

$= \{2, 3, \underline{4}, 5, \underline{1}, 6, 7\}/\{1, 4, 8\}$

$= \{2, 3, 5, 6, 7\}$

$\Rightarrow$ # $(A \cup B)/C = 5$

(vii) $\underline{\text{Find # } (A \cup B \cup C)'}$

$(A \cup B \cup C)' = \{9\}$

$\Rightarrow$ # $(A \cup B \cup C)' = 1$

Section G
Written Problems

30 people were asked which Irish TV station they preferred.

11 preferred RTE1.

12 preferred RTE2.

16 preferred TV3.

3 liked both RTE1 and RTE2.

6 liked both RTE2 and TV3.

4 liked both RTE1 and TV3.

If 2 liked all 3 stations, draw a Venn diagram to show the above information and hence calculate how many said that they liked none of the three stations.

Again, we will complete the Venn diagram *from the middle out*.

① 2 liked all three TV stations.

[30]

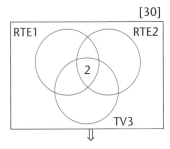

② 3 liked RTE1 and RTE2 [3 – 2 = 1]

[30]

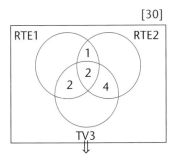

- 6 liked RTE2 and TV3 [6 – 2 = 4]
- 4 liked RTE1 and TV3 [4 – 2 = 2]

③ [30]

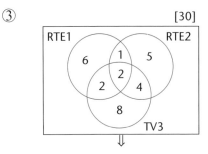

- 11 preferred RTE1

  11 – (2 + 2 + 1) = 6
- 12 preferred RTE2

  12 – (1 + 2 + 4) = 5
- 16 preferred TV3

  16 – (2 + 2 + 4) = 8

How many liked none of the channels?

[30]

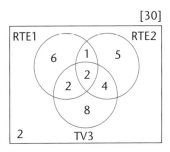

$$6 + 2 + 2 + 1 + 5 + 4 + 8 = 28$$
$$30 - 28 = \underline{2}$$

So, 2 people liked none of the channels.

Chapter 1

Sample questions for you to try

Question 1

(a) In a survey, 18 people were asked to name their favourite drink. 10 said they liked Coke, 12 said they liked Fanta while 7 said they liked both drinks. Draw a Venn diagram to illustrate the information above. Hence, calculate how many liked neither drink.

(b)

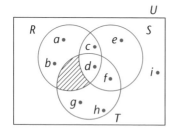

From the diagram above, list the elements of:

(i) $R \cup S$

(ii) $R \cap S \cap T$

(iii) $R/(S \cup T)$

(iv) $(R \cup T)/S$

(v) $(R \cup T)'$ `

(vi) Find # $(R \cup T \cup S)'$

(vii) Find # $(R \cap S)$

Question 2

(a) Complete the Venn diagram below to illustrate the following information:

$A = \{m, n, p, r\}$

$B = \{p, f, g\}$

$U = \{m, n, p, g, f, r, h, i\}$

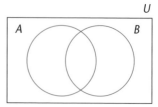

Use your diagram to find the elements of:

(i) $A \cap B$

(ii) B/A

(iii) A'

(iv) Find # $(A \cup B)'$

(b) In a particular class, 18 study French, 10 study German while 4 study neither language. If there are 28 in the class, draw a Venn diagram to illustrate the above information and calculate how many study both French and German.

(c) Copy the Venn diagram below and use separate diagrams to shade each of the following:

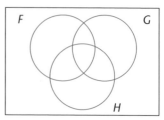

(i) $(F \cup G)'$

(ii) $(F \cup H)/G$

(iii) $H/(F \cup G)$

Question 3

(a) 24 people were asked what their favourite sport was. The results are shown below:

[24]

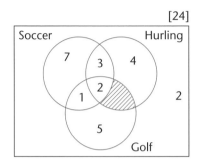

How many said they liked:

- **(i)** Golf only.
- **(ii)** Soccer and Hurling.
- **(iii)** Hurling and Soccer but not Golf.
- **(iv)** Soccer.

(b)

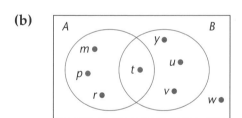

Say whether each of the following statements are true or false:

- **(i)** $r \subset A$
- **(ii)** $\{t\} \subset B$
- **(iii)** $A = B$
- **(iv)** $\{v\} \in B$
- **(v)** $\{m, t, r, p\} = A$
- **(vi)** $v \notin A$

Solution to question 1

(a) [18]

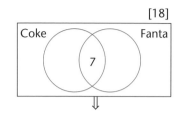

7 said they like both drinks

[18]

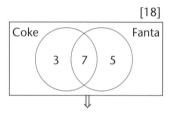

- 10 like Coke [10 − 7 = 3]
- 12 like Fanta [12 − 7 = 5]

[18]

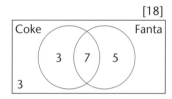

$3 + 7 + 5 = 15$

$18 - 15 = \underline{3}$

Therefore 3 people like neither drink.

(b)

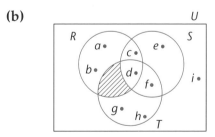

- **(i)** $R \cup S = \underline{\{a, b, c, d, e, f\}}$
- **(ii)** $R \cap S \cap T = \{d\}$
- **(iii)** $R/(S \cup T)$

$= \{a, b, c, d\}/\{c, e, d, f, g, h\}$

$= \underline{\{a, b\}}$

(iv) $(R \cup T)/S$

$\{a, b, \underline{c}, \underline{d}, g, h, f\}/\{c, e, d, f\}$

$= \underline{\{a, b, g, h\}}$

(v) $(R \cup T)'$

All elements outside $R \cap T$

$= \underline{\{e, i\}}$

(vi) Find $\#(R \cup T \cup S)'$

$(R \cup T \cup S)' = \{i\}$

$\Rightarrow \quad \# (R \cup T \cup S)' = 1$

(vii) Find $\# (R \cap S)$

$(R \cap S) = \{c, d\}$

$\Rightarrow \quad \# (R \cap S) = 2$

Solution to question 2

(a) $A = \{m, n, p, r\}$

$B = \{p, f, g\}$

$U = \{m, n, p, g, f, r, h, i\}$

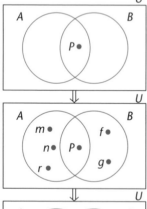

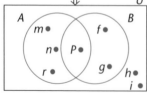

(i) $A \cap B = \{p\}$

(ii) $B/A = \{f, g\}$

(iii) $A' = \{f, g, h, i\}$

(iv) Find $\# (A \cup B)'$

$(A \cup B)' = \{h, i\}$

$\Rightarrow \quad \# (A \cup B)' = 2$

(b) [28]

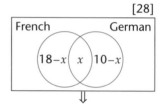

① We don't know how many study both subjects.

[28]

② • 18 study French
   • 10 study German

[28]

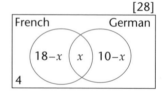

③ 4 study neither language.

Evaluate x

$4 + (18 - x) + x + (10 - x) = 28$

$4 + 18 - x + x + 10 - x = 28$

$32 - x = 28 \quad \Rightarrow \underline{x = 4}$

So, 4 study both languages.

(c)

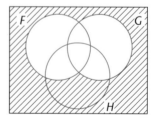

(i) $(F \cup G)'$

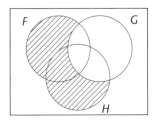

(ii) $(F \cup H)/G$

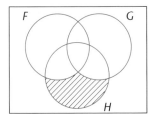

(iii) $H/(F \cup G)$

Solution to question 3

(a)   [24]

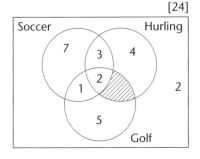

(i)   5 like Golf only.

(ii) 5 like Soccer and Hurling.

(iii) 3 like Hurling and Soccer but not Golf.

(iv) 13 like Soccer.

(b)

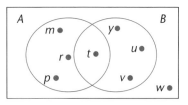

(i) $r \subset A$

This is *false*: because as r is not in brackets, it is an element and not a set.

(ii) $\{t\} \subset B$

This is *true*.

(iii) $A = B$

This is *false*. For two sets to be equal, they must have exactly the same elements.

(iv) $\{v\} \in B$

This is *false* because $\{v\}$ is a set, not an element.

(v) $\{m,\ t,\ r,\ p\} = A$

This is *true*.

(iv) $v \notin A$

This is *true* because $v \in B$ only.

Chapter 2
Arithmetic

Section A
Ratio and Proportions

Example 1

Divide €2250 between John, Mary and Sheila in the ratio 2 : 3 : 4 respectively.

$$2 : 3 : 4$$

① **Add the ratios**

$$2 + 3 + 4 = 9$$

② **Make this the denominator in the case of each number.**

$$2 : 3 : 4$$

$$= \frac{2}{9} : \frac{3}{9} : \frac{4}{9}$$

③ Calculate $\frac{1}{9}$.

$$\begin{array}{r} 9\overline{\smash{\big)}\,2250} \\ \hline 250 \end{array} \quad \Rightarrow \quad \frac{1}{9} = €250$$

John	:	Mary	:	Sheila
2	:	3	:	4
$\frac{2}{9}$	:	$\frac{3}{9}$	:	$\frac{4}{9}$
(€250 × 2)	:	(€250 × 3)	:	(€250 × 4)
€500	:	€750	:	€1000

Check €500 + €750 + €1000

= €2250

Example 2

€x is divided between Bob, Sharon and Philip in the ratio 3 : 4 : 5 respectively. If Sharon receives €60, calculate how much Bob and Philip each received.

$$3 : 4 : 5$$
$$[3 + 4 + 5 = 12]$$

$$\Rightarrow \qquad \frac{3}{12} : \frac{4}{12} : \frac{5}{12}$$

Sharon received €60 = $\frac{4}{12}$

Important

$$€60 = \frac{4}{12}$$

* To find $\frac{1}{12}$, we divide by 4 and *not* 12. Please be clear about this.

$$€60 = \frac{4}{12}$$

$$\Rightarrow \ €60 \div 4 = €15 = \underline{\frac{1}{12}}$$

Bob	:	Sharon	:	Philip
3	:	4	:	5
$\frac{3}{12}$	:	$\frac{4}{12}$	:	$\frac{5}{12}$
(€15 × 3)	:	(€15 × 4)	:	(€15 × 5)
€45	:	€60	:	€75

Section B
Indices

Note 1

$$a^b \times a^c = a^{b+c}$$

$$\Rightarrow \quad 2^4 \times 2^5 = 2^9$$

Note 2

$$\frac{a^b}{a^c} = a^{b-c}$$

① $\Rightarrow \quad \dfrac{3^5}{3^2} = 3^{5-2} = 3^3$

② $\Rightarrow \quad \dfrac{4^4}{4^6} = 4^{4-6} = 4^{-2}$

Note 3

$$(a^b)^c = a^{b \times c}$$

$$\Rightarrow \quad (5^3)^2 = 5^6$$

Note 4

Using the calculator.
$$2^7 \rightarrow 2\,\boxed{y^x}\,7 = 128$$
(On a 'Casio' calculator use $\boxed{x^y}$.)

Example 1

Simplify $\dfrac{2^3 \times 2^5}{2^2 \times 2^3}$ giving your answer

in the form 2^n where $n \in N$.

$$\frac{2^3 \times 2^5}{2^2 \times 2^3} = \frac{2^{3+5}}{2^{2+3}} = \frac{2^8}{2^5} = 2^{8-5} = \boxed{2^3}$$

Example 2

Simplify $\dfrac{3^4 \times 3^3}{3^5 \times 3^4}$ giving your

answer in the form 3^n where $n \in z$.

$$\frac{3^4 \times 3^3}{3^5 \times 3^4} = \frac{3^{4+3}}{3^{5+4}} = \frac{3^7}{3^9} = 3^{7-9} = \boxed{3^{-2}}$$

Example 3

Evaluate t in each of the following:
(i) $(5^4)^2 = 5^t$
(ii) $625 = 5^t$

Solutions

(i) $\qquad (5^4)^2 = 5^{4 \times 2} = 5^8$

$\Rightarrow \qquad \underline{t = 8}$

(ii) $\qquad 625 = 5 \times 5 \times 5 \times 5$

$\qquad\qquad\qquad = 5^4$

> *To check*
>
> $$5^4 = 5\,\boxed{y^x}\,4 = 625$$

$\Rightarrow \qquad \underline{t = 4}$

Section C
Index Notation

Type 1

A number between 1 and 10 (but not 10)	$\times$	10^n (where n is a whole number)

We use Index Notation to express very large numbers as follows:

This is normally written as $a \times 10^n$ where $1 \leqslant a < 10$ and $n \in N$

Example 1

Express 3240 in the form
$a \times 10$ where $1 \leqslant a < 10$ and $n \in N$

Move the decimal point so that we end up with a number between 1 and 10.

$\Rightarrow$ $\qquad$ $3240.0 \to 3.240$

(We moved the decimal point 3 places to the left.)

So, $\qquad$ $\underline{3240 = 3.24 \times 10^3}$

Example 2

Express 861,240 in the form

$\qquad a \times 10^n$ where $1 \leq a < 10$

and $n \in N$.

$\qquad 861,240.0 \to 8.61240$

(We move the decimal point 5 places to give a number between 1 and 10.)

So, $\qquad 861,240 = \underline{8.6124 \times 10^5}$

Example 3

Evaluate $\dfrac{3512 \times 250}{439}$ and express

your answer in the form $a \times 10^n$ where $1 \leq a < 10$ and $n \in N$.

$$\frac{3512 \times 250}{439} = \frac{878,000}{439} = 2000$$

$$2000.0 \to 2.000$$

(We move the decimal point 3 places to give a number between 1 and 10.)

So, $\qquad \dfrac{3512 \times 250}{439} = 2 \times 10^3$

Type 2

Representing Index Notation on your calculator.

Numbers which are written in index notation are represented on the calculator using the *exponent* key.

$\quad$ This key is marked $\boxed{\text{Exp}}$ or $\boxed{EE}$ or $\boxed{E}$.

$\quad$ 3.71×10^5 is keyed into your calculator as follows: $3.71 \boxed{\text{Exp}} 5$

Important

If we press the $\boxed{=}$ key at the end, the calculator represents the number as a natural number.

$\qquad 3.71 \boxed{\text{Exp}} 5 = \underline{371,000}$

So, $\qquad 8.2 \times 10^3 \to 8.2 \boxed{\text{Exp}} 3$

$\qquad\qquad \boxed{=} \underline{8200}$

So, $\qquad 2.472 \times 10^4 \to 2.472 \boxed{\text{Exp}} 4$

$\qquad\qquad \boxed{=} \underline{24,720}$

Example 1

Express

(i) $3.8 \times 10^5 + 2.4 \times 10^3$

(ii) $4.1 \times 10^4 - 5.8 \times 10^2$

in the form $a \times 10^n$ where $1 \leq a < 10$ and $n \in Z$.

Important

In any question of this type follow these steps:

① $\;$ Represent each part as a natural number.

② $\;$ Evaluate the answer.

③ $\;$ Represent the answer in index notation.

(i) $3.8 \times 10^5 + 2.4 \times 10^3$

① *Write each part as a natural number*

$\qquad 3.8 \boxed{\text{Exp}} 5 \boxed{=} 380,000$

$\qquad 2.4 \boxed{\text{Exp}} 3 \boxed{=} 2400$

Therefore $3.8 \times 10^5 + 2.4 \times 10^3$

$\qquad\qquad = 380,000 + 2400$

② *Evaluate*

$\qquad\qquad = 380,000 + 2400 = 382,400$

③ Write the answer in index notation

$$382,400 \rightarrow 3.82400$$

(The decimal point was moved 5 places.)

So, $382,400 = 3.824 \times 10^5$

Therefore $3.8 \times 10^5 + 2.4 \times 10^3$

$$= 3.824 \times 10^5$$

(ii) **$4.1 \times 10^4 - 5.8 \times 10^2$**

$$4.1 \times 10^4 - 5.8 \times 10^2$$
$$= 41,000 - 580$$
$$= 40,420$$
$$= 4.042 \times 10^4$$

Example 2

Express

(i) $(2.1 \times 10^5) \times (3.5 \times 10^2)$

(ii) $(8.4 \times 10^6) \div (1.5 \times 10^3)$

(iii) $\dfrac{(4.2 \times 10^4) \times (2.5 \times 10^3)}{3.5 \times 10^2}$

in the form $a \times 10^n$ where $1 \leqslant a < 10$ and $n \in z$

(i) **$(2.1 \times 10^5) \times (3.5 \times 10^2)$**

$$(2.1 \times 10^5) \times (3.5 \times 10^2)$$
$$= 210,000 \times 350$$
$$= 73,500,000$$
$$= 7.35 \times 10^7$$

(ii) **$(8.4 \times 10^6) \div (1.5 \times 10^3)$**

$$(8.4 \times 10^6) \div (1.5 \times 10^3)$$
$$= 8,400,000 \div 1500$$
$$= 5600$$
$$= 5.6 \times 10^3$$

(iii) $\dfrac{(4.2 \times 10^4) \times (2.5 \times 10^3)}{3.5 \times 10^2}$

$$\frac{(4.2 \times 10^4) \times (2.5 \times 10^3)}{3.5 \times 10^2}$$

$$= \frac{42,000 \times 2500}{350} = \frac{105,000,000}{350}$$

$$= 300,000$$

$$= 3 \times 10^5$$

Section D
Estimation and Using the Calculator

In questions of this type we are first asked to estimate the answer to a problem before working out the correct answer on the calculator. **Both the estimation and the answer should be approximately equal.** If they are not, we know an error has been made and we check our work again.

Example 1

(i) Calculate an approximate value for $\dfrac{7.12 \times 3.9}{5.2}$

(ii) Using a calculator, or otherwise, calculate the exact value of

$$\frac{7.12 \times 3.9}{5.2}$$

(i) *Estimate the answer*
Round off each number to the nearest whole number.

$$\frac{7.12 \times 3.9}{5.2} = \frac{\boxed{7} \times \boxed{4}}{\boxed{5}}$$

Important
The answer *must* be estimated without the use of a calculator. All calculations must be shown clearly.

$$\frac{7 \times 4}{5} = \frac{28}{5} = 5.6$$

$$5\overline{)28.^300}$$
$$5.6$$

So, $\dfrac{7.12 \times 3.9}{5.2}$ is approximately equal to 5.6.

(ii) Using the calculator, evaluate the exact value of $\dfrac{7.12 \times 3.9}{5.2}$

> Always show the answer for top and bottom separately before evaluating the final answer.

$$\frac{7.12 \times 3.9}{5.2} = \frac{27.768}{5.2}$$
$$= \underline{5.34}$$

So, our exact value is 5.34. Again, it is important to check that the estimate and the exact value are close. This is the case here so there is no need to check our work again.

Example 2

(i) Estimate an approximate value for
$$\frac{\sqrt{35.7604} + 2.9 \times 1.95}{\sqrt{16.0801} + 1.19}$$

(ii) Using your calculator, or otherwise, find the exact answer.

(i) *Estimate*
Again, round all numbers off to the nearest whole number.
$$\frac{\sqrt{35.7604} + 2.9 \times 1.95}{\sqrt{16.0801} + 1.19}$$

$$= \frac{\sqrt{36} + 3 \times 2}{\sqrt{16} + 1}$$

$$= \frac{6 + 3 \times 2}{4 + 1}$$

> **Remember to work out any parts involving multiplication or division first.**

$$= \frac{6 + 6}{5} = \frac{12}{5} = 2.4$$

$$5\overline{)12.^200}$$
$$2.4$$

So, our approximate answer is $\underline{2.4}$.

(ii) *Exact value*
$$\frac{\sqrt{35.7604} + 2.9 \times 1.95}{\sqrt{16.0801} + 1.9}$$

Show the answer for the parts involving the square roots before proceeding.

$$= \frac{5.98 + 2.9 \times 1.95}{4.01 + 1.9}$$

$$= \frac{11.635}{5.2} = \underline{2.2375}$$

So, our exact answer is 2.2375 (which again, is quite close to our estimate).

Example 3

Evaluate $(2.3)^4 \times \dfrac{1}{3.4} + \sqrt{35.2}$ and give your answer correct to two decimal places.

> **Note 1**
> $$(2.3)^4 \rightarrow 2.3 \boxed{y^x} 4$$

> **Note 2**
> $$\frac{1}{3.4} \rightarrow 1 \boxed{a\,^b/_c} 3.4$$

So, $(2.3)^4 \times \dfrac{1}{3.4} + \sqrt{35.2}$

$= 2.3 \boxed{y^x} 4 \times 1 \boxed{a^{\,b}/_c} 3.4$

$+ \boxed{\sqrt{}} 35.2$

> **It is important to show the answer to each part before calculating the final answer.**

$= 5.29 \times 0.29411 + 5.9329$

$= 6.75602$

Therefore $(2.3)^4 \times \dfrac{1}{3.4} + \sqrt{35.2}$

$= \underline{6.76}$ correct to two decimal places.

Section E
Lowest Common Multiple (LCM) and Highest Common Factor (HCF)

Example 1

Calculate the Lowest Common Multiple, (LCM) of 2, 3 and 8.

> In the case of each number, list their multiples. The lowest common multiple is the lowest multiple which is in each list.

Multiples of 2 are 2, 4, 6, 8, 10, 12, 14, 16, 18, 20, 22, ㉔ . . .

Multiples of 3 are 3, 6, 9, 12, 15, 18, 21, ㉔, 27, 30 . . .

Multiples of 8 are 8, 16, ㉔, 32 . . .

As we can see, 24 is the Lowest Common Multiple because it is the smallest number which occurs in each list.

Example 2

Calculate the HCF Highest Common Factor of 30 and 18.

> In the case of each number, list their pairs of factors.
>
> The Highest Common Factor is the largest number which is a factor of both 30 and 18.

30	18
1×30	1×18
2×15	2×9
3×10	$3 \times ⑥$
$5 \times ⑥$	

As we can see, 6 is the Highest Common Factor because it is the largest number which is a factor of both 30 and 18.

Section F
Prime Factors

> **Remember**
>
> A prime number is a number whose only factors are 1 and itself,
>
> For example 2, 3, 5, 7, 11. . .

To find the prime factors of any number we *break down* the factors until nothing else can divide in.

Prime Factors of 12

So the prime factors of 12 are 2 and 3 as $12 = 2 \times 2 \times 3$

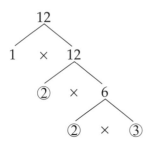

Important

1 is *not* a prime number so it is never listed as a prime factor.

Example

Find the prime factors of 36 and 60.

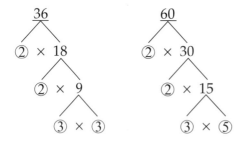

So, as $36 = 2 \times 2 \times 3 \times 3$ its prime factors are <u>2 and 3</u>.

Also, $60 = 2 \times 2 \times 3 \times 5$

Its prime factors are <u>2, 3 and 5</u>.

Section G
Compound Interest

With compound interest, the interest earned in year 1 is added to the principal in year 1 to give the principal at the start of year 2 and so on.

Example 1

€300 is lodged for two years at 4% compound interest. Calculate how much it amounts to at the end of that time.

Year 1

Start of year 1 = €300

Interest Earned

4% of €300   = €12

End of year 1 = €300 + €12

            = <u>€312</u>

Year 2

Start of year 2 = €312

Interest earned

4% of €312   = €12.48

End of year 2 = €312 + €12.48

            = <u>€324.48</u>

Therefore at the end of the second year there is €324.48 in the bank.

Example 2

Calculate the compound interest earned if €4000 is lodged for three years at 5% compound interest.

Year 1

Start €4000
Interest Earned
  5% of €4000 = €200
End
  €4000 + €200 = <u>€4200</u>

Year 2

Start €4200

Interest Earned

5% of €4200 = €210

End

€4200 + €210 = <u>€4410</u>

Year 3

Start €4410

Interest Earned

5% of €4410 = €220.50

End

€4410 + €220.50 = <u>€4630.50</u>

Calculate the interest earned

End year 3   = €4630.50
Start year 1 = €4000

Interest Earned € 630.50

Chapter 2
Sample questions for you to try

Question 1

(a) Simplify $\dfrac{4^4 \times 4^5}{4^2 \times 4^3}$ and express

your answer in the form 4^n where $n \in N$.

(b) (i) Find the Highest Common Factor (HCF) of 36, 24 and 72.

(ii) Find the Lowest Common Multiple (LCM) of 3, 8 and 12.

(c) €400 is divided between Michael, Tom and Barry in the ratio 2 : 3 : 5. Calculate how much each received.

(d) Calculate

$$\sqrt{31.2} - (2.6)^2 \times \frac{1}{41.3}$$

and express your answer to two decimal places.

Question 2

(a) List the prime factors of 42 and 80.

(b) Evaluate

$$\sqrt{42.4} + \frac{1}{2.7} \times (3.2)^5$$

correct to two decimal places.

(c) (i) Show how to calculate an approximate value for

$$\frac{3.2 \times 1.9}{3.8}$$

(ii) Using your calculator, or otherwise, evaluate the exact value.

(d) Simplify $\dfrac{2^6 \times 2^4}{2^3 \times 2}$ and express

your answer in the form 2^n where $n \in N$.

Question 3

(a) (i) Estimate an approximate

value for $\dfrac{(6.8)^2 + 5.26}{\sqrt{121.2201} - 3.01}$

(ii) Using your calculator, or otherwise, calculate the exact answer.

(b) Evaluate the following, expressing your answer in the form $a \times 10^n$ where $1 \leqslant a < 10$ and $n \in N$.

(i) 2.5×34.14

(ii) $3.6 \times 10^4 - 2.71 \times 10^2$

(iii) $\dfrac{2.4 \times 10^5}{9.6 \times 10^3}$

(c) €800 is lodged for three years at 10% compound interest. Calculate the amount of interest earned at the end of the three years.

Solution to question 1

(a) Simplify $\dfrac{4^4 \times 4^5}{4^2 \times 4^3}$

$$\frac{4^4 \times 4^5}{4^2 \times 4^3} = \frac{4^{4+5}}{4^{2+3}} = \frac{4^9}{4^5}$$

$$= 4^{9-5} = \underline{4^4}$$

(b)

(i) Find the HCF of 36, 24 and 72.

36	24	72
1×36	1×24	1×72
2×18	$2 \times ⑫$	2×36
$3 \times ⑫$	3×8	3×24
4×9	4×6	4×18
6×6		$6 \times ⑫$
		8×9

So, 12 is the Highest Common Factor as it is the largest number which is a factor of each.

(ii) Find the LCM of 3, 8 and 12.

Multiples of 3 are 3, 6, 9, 12, 15, 18, 21, ㉔, 27. . .

Multiples of 8 are 8, 16, ㉔, 32. . .

Multiples of 12 are 12, ㉔, 36, 48. . .

So, 24 is the LCM as it is the lowest multiple to appear in all three lists.

(c) €400 is divided between Michael, Tom and Barry in the ratio 2 : 3 : 5. How much did each receive?

Michael	:	Tom	:	Barry
2	:	3	:	5

$2 + 3 + 5 = 10$

Make this the denominator in each case.

$$\frac{2}{10} \quad : \quad \frac{3}{10} \quad : \quad \frac{5}{10}$$

Calculate $\dfrac{1}{10}$

$$\begin{array}{c|c} 10 & €\,400 \\ \hline & €\,40 \end{array} \quad \Rightarrow \quad €40 = \frac{1}{10}$$

Michael	:	Tom	:	Barry
$\frac{2}{10}$	:	$\frac{3}{10}$	:	$\frac{5}{10}$

$$(€40 \times 2) \;:\; (€40 \times 3) : \;(€40 \times 5)$$
$$€80 \quad : \quad €120 \quad : \quad €200$$

So, Michael received €80,
  Tom received €120,
  Barry received €200.

(d) Calculate $\sqrt{31.2} - (2.6)^2 \times \dfrac{1}{41.3}$
correct to 2 decimal places.

$\boxed{\sqrt{}}\ 31.2 - (2.6)\ \boxed{x^2}\ \times 1\ \boxed{a\ ^b/_c}\ 41.3$

$= 5.5857 - 6.76 \times 0.0242$

$= 5.42201563$

$= 5.42$ correct to 2 decimal places

22

Solution to question 2

(a) List the prime factors of 42 and 80.

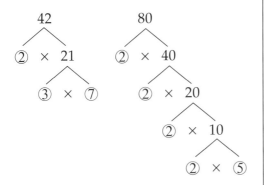

$42 = 2 \times 3 \times 7$

So, the prime factors of 42 are 2, 3 and 7.

$80 = 2 \times 2 \times 2 \times 2 \times 5$

So, the prime factors of 80 are 2 and 5.

(b) Evaluate $\sqrt{42.4} + \dfrac{1}{2.7} \times (3.2)^5$ correct to two decimal places.

$\boxed{\sqrt{\ }}\ 42.4 + 1\ \boxed{a\,^b/_c}\ 2.7 \times 3.2\ \boxed{y^x}\ 5$

$= 6.51153 + 0.37037 \times 335.544$

$= 130.7872$

$= \underline{130.79}$ correct to 2 decimal places

(c)

(i) Estimate $\dfrac{3.2 \times 1.9}{3.8}$

$\dfrac{3.2 \times 1.9}{3.8} = \dfrac{\boxed{3} \times \boxed{2}}{\boxed{4}}$

$= \dfrac{6}{4} = \underline{1.5}$

$\begin{array}{r} 4\,\overline{|6.^200} \\ \hline 1.5 \end{array}$ Again, it's important to show this.

(ii) Calculate t he exact value of $\dfrac{3.2 \times 1.9}{3.8}$

Again, show the answer for the multiplication part before finding a final answer.

$$\frac{3.2 \times 1.9}{3.8} = \frac{6.08}{3.8}$$

$$= \underline{1.6}$$

These answers are close to each other so there is no real need to check our work again.

(d) Simplify $\dfrac{2^6 \times 2^4}{2^3 \times 2}$ and express your answer in the form 2^n where $n \in N$.

Note $2 = 2^1$

So, $\dfrac{2^6 \times 2^4}{2^3 \times 2^1} = \dfrac{2^{6+4}}{2^{3+1}} = \dfrac{2^{10}}{2^4}$

$= 2^{10-4} = 2^6$

Solution to question 3

(a)

(i) Estimate $\dfrac{(6.8)^2 + 5.26}{\sqrt{121.2201} - 3.01}$

Again, round each number up or down to the nearest whole number.

$\Rightarrow \quad \dfrac{7^2 + 5}{\sqrt{121} - 3} = \dfrac{49 + 5}{11 - 3}$

$$\frac{54}{8} = \underline{6.75} \uparrow$$

$$8 \overline{)54.^60^400}$$
$$6.75$$

(ii) Calculate the exact value.

$$\frac{(6.8)^2 + 5.26}{\sqrt{121.2201} - 3.01}$$

We show we can correctly evaluate $(6.8)^2$ and $\sqrt{121.2201}$ before continuing.

$$\frac{46.24 + 5.26}{11.01 - 3.01} = \frac{51.5}{8}$$

$$= \underline{6.4375}$$

(b) Express the following in the form $a \times 10^n$ where $1 \leqslant a < 10$ and $n \in N$.

(i)   **2.5 × 34.14**

         = 85.35

$85.35 \rightarrow 8.535$

We move the decimal point 1 place to give a number between 1 and 10.

$\Rightarrow$ $2.5 \times 34.14 = \underline{8.535 \times 10^1}$

(ii)   **$3.6 \times 10^4 - 2.71 \times 10^2$**

         $= 36{,}000 - 271$

         $= 35{,}729$

         $= \underline{3.5729 \times 10^4}$

(iii) $\boxed{\dfrac{2.4 \times 10^5}{9.6 \times 10^3}}$

     $= \dfrac{240{,}000}{9600} = 25$

     $= \underline{2.5 \times 10'}$

(c) €800 is lodged for 3 years at 10% compound interest.

$\boxed{\text{Year 1}}$

Start €800

Interest Earned

    10% of €800 = €80

End

    €800 + €80 = €880

$\boxed{\text{Year 2}}$

Start €880

Interest Earned

    10% of €880 = €88

End

    €880 + €88 = €968

$\boxed{\text{Year 3}}$

Start €968

Interest Earned

    10% of €968 = €96.80

End

    €968 + €96.80 = €1064.80

Calculate the interest earned.

$\Rightarrow$ Interest earned = €1064.80 − €800

                 = €264.80

Chapter 3
Percentages

Section A
Cost Price, Selling Price, Percentage Profit

There are two very important things to understand which relate to this section.

Note 1

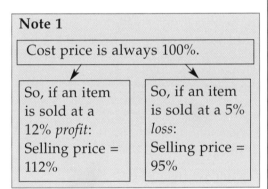

Cost price is always 100%.

| So, if an item is sold at a 12% *profit*: Selling price = 112% | So, if an item is sold at a 5% *loss*: Selling price = 95% |

Example

John sells a coat for €102 which represents a 15% loss on the original cost price.

Calculate

(i) The cost price of the coat.

(ii) The selling price of the coat if it were sold for a 22% profit.

(i) Selling price = €102

$$= 15\% \text{ loss}$$

$$\Rightarrow \text{Selling price} = 85\% \ (100\% - 15\%)$$

> *Always* calculate 1% first.

$$€102 = 85\%$$

$$€\frac{102}{85} = 1\%$$

$$€1.2 = 1\%$$

$$\text{Cost price} = 100\%$$

$$= €1.2 \times 100$$

$$= \underline{€120}$$

(ii) Cost price = €120

$$\underline{\text{So } €120 = 100\%}$$

Sold at 22% profit

So, *Selling price* = 122%

> Again, always evaluate 1% first.

$$€120 = 100\%$$

$$\frac{€120}{100} = 1\%$$

$$€1.2 = 1\%$$

$$\text{Selling price} = 122\%$$

$$= €1.2 \times 122$$

$$= \underline{€146.40}$$

Note 2

$$\frac{\text{Percentage}}{\text{Profit}} = \frac{\text{Profit}}{\text{Cost price}} \times \frac{100}{1}$$

Example 1

Sheila buys a car for €8000 and later sells the same car for €9000. Calculate her percentage profit.

Cost price = €8000.

Selling price = €9000.

$\Rightarrow$ Profit = €1000

So, percentage profit

$$= \frac{\text{Profit}}{\text{Cost price}} \times \frac{100}{1}$$

$$= \frac{1000}{8000} \times \frac{100}{1} = \underline{12.5\%}$$

$\Rightarrow$ Percentage profit = 12.5%

Example 2

Mary buys four rings. The individual costs of the rings were €80, €70, €110 and €40.

A year later the rings were sold at an average price of €66.

Calculate Mary's percentage loss on the transaction.

Cost price = €80 + €70 + €110 + €40

= €300

Selling price = €66 × 4

= €264

*As the selling price is lower than the cost price, a *loss* is made.

Loss = €300 − €264

= €36

Percentage loss = $\dfrac{\text{Loss}}{\text{Cost price}} \times \dfrac{100}{1}$

$$= \frac{36}{300} \times \frac{100}{1} = \underline{12\%}$$

So, the percentage loss is 12%.

The following two notes are also very important. Please read them carefully.

Note 1

When a question involves an amount of money being lodged for 1 year only...

Amount at the start of the year is always 100%.

⇓

€250 is lodged at r% interest.

start of year [€250] = 100%

↓ r% interest

end of year [ ] = (100 + r)%

Example 1

€400 is lodged at 6% interest. How much is in the bank at the end of the year?

start of year [€400] = 100%

↓ 6% interest

end of year [x] = 106%

€400 = 100%

Again *always* evaluate 1% first

€400 ÷ 100 = 1%

€4 = 1%

x = 106%

= €4 × 106 = €424

So, there was €424 at the end of the year.

Example 2

A certain amount of money was lodged at 16% interest. Calculate how much was lodged if there was €278.40 in the bank at the end ot the year.

start of year $\boxed{x}$ = 100%

16% interest

end of year $\boxed{€278.40}$ = 116%

$$€278.40 = 116\%$$

$$\frac{€278.40}{116} = 1\%$$

$\Rightarrow$ $€2.4 = 1\%$

$$x = 100\% = €2.4 \times 100$$

$$= \underline{€240}$$

So, €240 was lodged at the start of the year.

Note 2

$$\text{Interest Rate} = \frac{\text{Amount of interest}}{\substack{\text{Amount at the} \\ \text{start of the year}}} \times \frac{100}{1}$$

Example

€700 is lodged in the bank. Calculate the rate of interest earned if there is €868 in the bank at the end of the year.

start of year $\boxed{€700}$

r% interest

end of year $\boxed{€868}$

Interest earned

$$= €868 - €700$$

$$= \underline{€168}$$

$$\text{Interest Rate} = \frac{\text{Amount of interest}}{\substack{\text{Amount at the} \\ \text{start of the year}}} \times \frac{100}{1}$$

$$= \frac{168}{700} \times \frac{100}{1} = \underline{24\%}$$

So, the interest rate for the year was 24%.

Section C
Value Added Tax (VAT)

The following must be clearly understood before attempting any question involving VAT.

Note 1

If the cost of an item does not include VAT, let the cost equal 100%.

$\boxed{\text{A bike costs } €x \text{ which does not include VAT.}}$ $\longrightarrow$ $€x = 100\%$

If the cost of an item includes r% VAT, let the cost equal (100 + r)%.

$\boxed{\text{A coat costs } €y \text{ which includes 8% VAT.}}$ $\longrightarrow$ $€y = 108\%$

Example

A car costs €14,880 which includes 24% VAT. Calculate:

(i) The cost of the car without VAT.

(ii) How much would the car cost if the amount of VAT were reduced to 15%?

27

(i) Find the cost without VAT.

Car costs €14,880 which includes 24% VAT. → €14,880 = 124%

Again, always find 1% first

$$€14,880 = 124\%$$

$$\frac{€14,880}{124} = 1\%$$

$$\Rightarrow \qquad €120 = 1\%$$

Find cost without VAT

Cost without VAT = 100%

$$= €120 \times 100$$

$$= €12,000$$

(ii) How much would the car cost with 15% VAT?

Cost with 15% VAT → let cost = 115%

$$€120 = 1\%$$

$$€120 \times 115 = 115\%$$

$$€13,800 = 115\%$$

So, cost with 15% VAT = €13,800.

Note 2

$$\frac{\text{Percentage}}{\text{VAT}} = \frac{\text{Amount of VAT}}{\text{Cost without VAT}} \times \frac{100}{1}$$

Example

The cost of a book, without VAT, is €80. When VAT is added the cost increases to €92. Calculate the percentage VAT added.

$$\text{Cost with VAT} = €92$$
$$- \text{Cost without VAT} = €80$$
$$\overline{\qquad\qquad\qquad\qquad\qquad}$$
$$\Rightarrow \qquad \text{Amount of VAT} = \underline{€12}$$

$$\frac{\text{Percentage}}{\text{VAT}} = \frac{\text{Amount of VAT}}{\text{Cost without VAT}} \times \frac{100}{1}$$

$$\Rightarrow \qquad \%\text{VAT} = \frac{12}{80} \times \frac{100}{1}$$

$$= 15\%$$

So, the percentage VAT is 15%.

Section D
Income Tax

Note 1

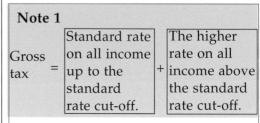

Gross tax	=	Standard rate on all income up to the standard rate cut-off.	+	The higher rate on all income above the standard rate cut-off.

'Standard rate cut-off = €10,000
Standard tax rate = 15%
Higher tax rate = 20%
Total wage = €18,000'
⇓

Gross tax	=	Standard rate on all income up to the standard rate cut-off.	+	Higher rate on all income above the standard rate cut-off.

$$\frac{\text{Gross}}{\text{Tax}} = \boxed{15\% \text{ of } €10,000} + \boxed{20\% \text{ of } €8000}$$

Please read through this carefully until you understand it fully.

Example

Cian has a gross yearly income of €22,500. He has a standard rate cut-off of €18,000. His standard rate of tax is 12% and his higher rate is 16%. Calculate his gross tax.

Standard rate cut-off = €18,000

Standard tax rate = 12%

Higher tax rate = 16%

Gross wage = €22,500

Gross Tax = $\boxed{\text{12% of €18,000}}$ + $\boxed{\text{16% of €4500}}$

(€22,500 – €18,000 = €4500)

12% of €18,000 = €2160

16% of €4500 = €720

⇒ Gross Tax = $\boxed{\text{€2160}}$ + $\boxed{\text{€720}}$

= €2880

Note 2

$\boxed{\text{Gross Tax – Tax credits = Tax paid}}$

Gross wage = €25,000
Gross Tax   = €6300
Tax credits = €2000

⇓

$\boxed{\text{Gross Tax – Tax credits = Tax paid}}$

⇒   €6300 – €2000 = Tax paid

€4300 = Tax paid

Nett *wage* = Gross wage – Tax paid

⇒ Nett wage = €25,000 – €4300

= €20,700

Example 1

David has a gross wage of €30,000 and a standard rate cut-off of €33,000. His standard rate of tax is 14%. David has a tax credit of €2000.

Calculate:

(i) His gross tax.

(ii) The total amount of tax he paid.

(iii) His nett wage.

(i) *Calculate his gross tax.*

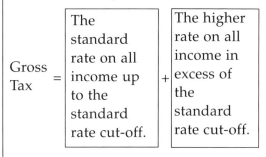

Gross Tax =	The standard rate on all income up to the standard rate cut-off.	+	The higher rate on all income in excess of the standard rate cut-off.

Gross Tax = $\boxed{\text{14% of €30,000}}$ + $\boxed{0}$

↑

David's income does not exceed the standard rate cut-off so all of his income is taxed at the standard rate.

$\boxed{\text{Gross Tax = 14% of €30,000}}$

= €4200

(ii) *Calculate the total amount of tax paid.*

$\boxed{\text{Gross Tax – Tax credits = Tax paid}}$

⇒   €4200 – €2000 = Tax paid

⇒   €2200 = *Tax paid*

(iii) *Calculate his nett wage.*

$\boxed{\text{Nett wage = Gross wage – Tax paid}}$

⇒ Nett wage = €30,000 – €2200

= €27,800

Example 2

Lisa earns a gross yearly wage of €43,000 and has a standard rate cut-off of €32,000. Her standard rate of tax is 16% and her higher rate is 24%. If Lisa has a tax credit of €3500, calculate:

(i) Her gross tax.

(ii) The total amount of tax she pays.

(iii) Her nett wage.

(i) *Calculate her gross tax.*

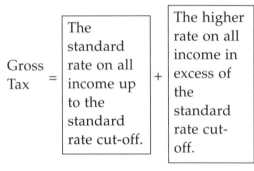

$$\Rightarrow \quad \frac{\text{Gross}}{\text{Tax}} = \boxed{\begin{array}{c}16\% \text{ of}\\ €32{,}000\end{array}} + \boxed{\begin{array}{c}24\% \text{ of}\\ €11{,}000\end{array}}$$
↑

(€43,000 − €32,000 = €11,000)

$\Rightarrow \qquad$ Gross Tax = €5120 + €2640

$\qquad\qquad\quad = \underline{€7760}$

(ii) *Calculate the total amount of tax Lisa pays.*

Gross Tax − Tax credit = Tax paid

$\Rightarrow \qquad$ €7760 − €3500 = Tax paid

$\Rightarrow \qquad$ €4260 = Tax paid

(iii) *Calculate her nett wage.*

Nett wage = Gross wage − Tax paid

$\Rightarrow$ Nett wage = €43,000 − €4260

$\qquad\qquad = \underline{€38{,}740}$

Note 3

$$\frac{\text{Rate of}}{\text{Tax}} = \frac{\text{Gross Tax}}{\text{Gross Income}} \times \frac{100}{1}$$

The following example is quite difficult but with practice you will find it very manageable.

Example

Yvonne earns a gross wage of €32,000 and has a standard rate cut-off of €38,000. She has a tax credit of €2000 and pays €3120 in tax. Calculate her standard tax rate.

Gross Tax − Tax credits = Tax paid

$\Rightarrow \qquad$ Gross Tax − €2000 = €3120

$\Rightarrow \qquad$ Gross Tax = €3120 + €2000

$\qquad\qquad$ Gross Tax = €5120

$$\frac{\text{Rate of}}{\text{Tax}} = \frac{\text{Gross Tax}}{\text{Gross Income}} \times \frac{100}{1}$$

$\Rightarrow \qquad \dfrac{\text{Rate of}}{\text{Tax}} = \dfrac{5120}{32{,}000} \times \dfrac{100}{1}$

$\qquad\qquad = \underline{16\%}$

So, her standard rate of tax is 16%.

Section E
Distance, Speed, Time

The triangle below is quite well known but very important for remembering the three formulas involving Distance, Speed and Time.

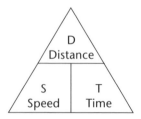

By covering over the quantity required (D, S or T) any of the formulas below can be found by inspection:

① $S = \dfrac{D}{T} \rightarrow$ $\boxed{\textbf{Speed} = \dfrac{\textbf{Distance}}{\textbf{Time}}}$

② $T = \dfrac{D}{S} \rightarrow$ $\boxed{\textbf{Time} = \dfrac{\textbf{Distance}}{\textbf{Speed}}}$

③ $D = S \times T \rightarrow$ $\boxed{\textbf{Distance} = \textbf{Speed} \times \textbf{Time}}$

Example 1

A car leaves Cork at 1140 hrs and arrives in Dublin at 1510 hrs. Calculate the average speed of the car in km/hr if the total journey length is 315 km.

- Distance = <u>315 km</u>

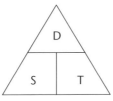

- Calculating time taken

1510 hrs		15 hrs 10 min
<u>1140 hrs</u>	$\Rightarrow$	<u>11 hrs 40 min</u>

*We cannot take 40 min from 10 min so

15 hrs 10 min → 14 hrs 70 min

– We take one hour away from the 15 hrs.

– We add that hour (60 minutes) onto the 10 min.

$$\begin{array}{r} 14 \text{ hrs } 70 \text{ min} \\ - 11 \text{ hrs } 40 \text{ min} \\ \hline 3 \text{ hrs } 30 \text{ min} \end{array}$$

Very important

We must *always* express time as a decimal.

– 15 minutes = $\dfrac{1}{4}$ hour = 0.25 hour

– 30 minutes = $\dfrac{1}{2}$ hour = 0.5 hour

– 45 minutes = $\dfrac{3}{4}$ hour = 0.75 hour

Therefore time taken = <u>3.5 hrs</u>

Calculate average speed

$$\textbf{Speed} = \dfrac{\textbf{Distance}}{\textbf{Time}}$$

$\Rightarrow$ $\qquad$ Speed $= \dfrac{315}{3.5}$

$\qquad\qquad$ $= 90$

So, average speed = <u>90 km/hr</u>

Example 2

Calculate, in hours and minutes, the time taken for a man to run a race of 51 km in length at an average speed of 12 km/hr.

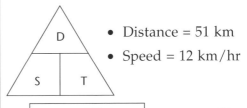

- Distance = 51 km
- Speed = 12 km/hr

$\boxed{\textbf{Time} = \dfrac{\textbf{Distance}}{\textbf{Speed}}} \Rightarrow$ Time $= \dfrac{51}{12}$

$\qquad\qquad$ = 4.25 hrs

$\Rightarrow$ Time $= 4.25$ hours

$\qquad\qquad$ $= 4\dfrac{1}{4}$ hours

$\qquad\qquad$ = <u>4 hours 15 minutes</u>

Example 3

A train departs Galway station at 0950 hrs and arrives in Mallow station at 1235 hrs. If the average speed of the train during the journey was 120 km/hr, calculate the distance travelled.

- Speed = 120 km/hr
- *Calculate time*

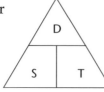

$$\begin{array}{c} 12 \text{ hrs } 35 \text{ min} \\ - 9 \text{ hrs } 50 \text{ min} \\ \hline \end{array} \Rightarrow \begin{array}{c} 11 \text{ hrs } 95 \text{ min} \\ - 9 \text{ hrs } 50 \text{ min} \\ \hline 2 \text{ hrs } 45 \text{ min} \end{array}$$

$\Rightarrow$ Time taken $= 2 \text{ hrs } 45 \text{ min}$

$$= 2\frac{3}{4} \text{ hrs}$$

$$= \underline{2.75 \text{ hrs}}$$

$$\boxed{\textbf{Distance = Speed} \times \textbf{Time}}$$

$$\Downarrow$$

$$\text{Distance} = 120 \times 2.75$$

$$= 330 \text{ km}$$

So, the distance travelled was

$$= \underline{330 \text{ km}}$$

Question 1

(a) George has a gross annual wage of €28,000 and a standard rate cut-off of €30,000. He has a tax credit of €2700. If his standard rate of tax is 26%. Calculate:

(i) His total tax paid.

(ii) His nett wage.

(b) Michelle sells a bike for €153 which represents a 15% loss on the original cost price. Calculate:

(i) The cost price of the bike.

(ii) What the percentage profit would be if the bike was sold for €200.

(c) A car travelled $121\frac{1}{2}$ miles in one day. It commenced its journey at 1230 hrs and finished at 1445 hrs. Calculate the average speed of the car, in km/hr.

Question 2

(a) A train completed a journey of 315 km at an average speed of 140 km/hr. Calculate the time taken, in hours and minutes, to complete the journey.

(b) €1200 is lodged at the start of the year at $r\%$ interest. If there was €1296 at the end of the year, calculate 'r'.

(c) Breda earns €300 a week and has a tax credit of €20. If her tax rate is 14%, complete the table below:

Gross pay ☐

14% tax ☐

Tax credit €20

Tax paid ☐

Take-home pay ☐

Question 3

(a) An amount of money is lodged at 14% interest. If there is €31.92 in the bank at the end of the year, calculate how much was lodged.

(b) At 0850 hrs Tom started to cycle around his home town of Tuam. He cycled at an average speed of 18 km/hr and finished the journey at 1520 hrs. Calculate the total length of his trip that day.

(c) A watch costs €70 before VAT is included and costs €79.80 after VAT is added. Evaluate:

(i) The percentage of VAT added.

(ii) The cost of the watch if 34% VAT was included.

Solution to question 1

(a)
> **Gross Wage = €28,000**
> **Standard rate cut-off = €30,000**
> **Tax credit = €2700**
> **Standard tax rate = 26%**

(i) *Calculate his total tax paid.*

Gross Tax = 26% of €28,000 + 0

= €7280

Again, because he did not earn anything in excess of his standard rate cut-off, all his wage is taxed at the standard rate.

> Gross Tax – Tax credit = Tax paid

€7280 – €2700 = Tax paid

$\Rightarrow$ €4580 = Tax paid

(ii) *Calculate his nett wage.*

> Take-home pay (nett wage) = Gross wage – Tax paid

$\Rightarrow$ Nett wage = €28,000 – €4580

= €23,420

(b)
> **A bike is sold for €153, a 15% loss.**

(i) Calculate the cost price of the bike.

€153 represents a 15% loss

$\Rightarrow$ €153 = 85% (100% – 15%)

> Cost price is always 100%

Always find 1% first.

€153 = 85%

$\dfrac{€153}{85} = 1\%$

€1.8 = 1%

€1.8 × 100 = 100%

$\Rightarrow$ €180 = 100%

So, cost price is €180

> **(ii) What would the percentage profit be if the bike was sold for €200?**

$$\boxed{\% \text{ profit} = \frac{\text{profit}}{\text{Cost price}} \times \frac{100}{1}}$$

- Cost price = €180

⇒ If the bike was sold for €200, the profit would be €20.

$$\Rightarrow \% \text{ profit} = \frac{20}{180} \times \frac{100}{1}$$

$$= \underline{11.11\%}$$

(c)

- Distance = <u>121.5 km</u>

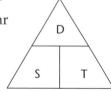

Calculate time taken

14 hrs 45 min

− 12 hrs 30 min

2 hrs 15 min $= 2\frac{1}{4}$ hours

$= 2.25$ hours

$$\boxed{\text{Speed} = \frac{\text{Distance}}{\text{Time}}} \Rightarrow \text{Speed} = \frac{121.5}{2.25}$$

$$= \underline{54}$$

So, the car travelled at an average speed of 54 km/hr.

Solution to question 2

(a) A train travels 315 km at 140 km/hr. Calculate the time taken.

- Distance = 315 km
- Speed = 140 km/hr

$$\boxed{\text{Time} = \frac{\text{Distance}}{\text{Speed}}} \Rightarrow \text{Time} = \frac{315}{140}$$

$$= 2.25$$

So, time taken = 2.25 hours

$$= 2\frac{1}{4} \text{ hours}$$

$$= \underline{2 \text{ hours } 15 \text{ minutes}}$$

(b) €1200 is lodged at *r*% interest. There is €1296 at the end of the year. Find *r*.

start of year €1200

  ↓ *r*%

end of year €1296

$$\frac{\text{Rate of}}{\text{Interest}} = \frac{\text{Amount of Interest}}{\begin{array}{c}\text{Amount at the start}\\ \text{of the year}\end{array}} \times \frac{100}{1}$$

$$\frac{\text{Rate of}}{\text{Interest}} = \frac{96}{1200} \times \frac{100}{1}$$

$$= \underline{8\%}$$

(c) Gross pay €300

14% tax €42 → 14% of €300

Tax credit €20

Tax paid €22 → Gross tax − tax credit

Take-home pay €278 →

Gross Wage − Tax paid = Nett wage

(€300 − €22)

Solution to question 3

(a) An amount of money is lodged at 14% interest. If there is €31.92 at the end of the year find how much was lodged.

start of year $\boxed{x}$ Always 100%

↓ 14% interest

end of year $\boxed{\text{€31.92}}$ 114%

€31.92 = 114%

Again always find 1%.

$$\frac{€31.92}{114} = 1\%$$

⇒   €0.28 = 1%

Find x

€0.28 × 100 = 100%

⇒ $\underline{€28 = 100\%}$

So, €28 was lodged.

(b) • Speed = 18 km/hr

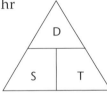

Calculate time taken.

$$\begin{array}{c} 15 \text{ hrs } 20 \text{ min} \\ - 08 \text{ hrs } 50 \text{ min} \end{array} \Rightarrow \begin{array}{c} 14 \text{ hrs } 80 \text{ min} \\ - 08 \text{ hrs } 50 \text{ min} \end{array}$$

6 hrs 30 min

⇒ Time taken = $6\frac{1}{2}$ hours

= 6.5 hours

$\boxed{\text{Distance} = \text{Speed} \times \text{Time}}$

Distance = 18 × 6.5

= 117

So, distance = $\underline{117 \text{ km}}$

(c) $\boxed{\begin{array}{l} \textbf{Cost without VAT = €70} \\ \textbf{Cost including VAT = €79.80} \end{array}}$

(i) Find the percentage VAT.

$\boxed{\% \text{ VAT} = \dfrac{\text{Amount of VAT}}{\text{Cost without VAT}} \times \dfrac{100}{1}}$

$$\% \text{ VAT} = \frac{9.80}{70} \times \frac{100}{1}$$

$$= \underline{14\%}$$

(ii) The cost of the watch if 34% VAT is added.

Cost without VAT   = €70

34% of €70   = €23.80
(added VAT)

⇒ Cost including 34% VAT = $\underline{€93.80}$

35

Chapter **4**
Algebra

Section A
Simple Equations

Important

In any equation containing only x terms and numbers we *must* rearrange as folows:

$$\boxed{x \text{ terms}} \;=\; \boxed{\text{numbers}}$$

Example 1

Solve $-2x + 4 = 3x - 6$

① *Rearrange correctly.*

$$\boxed{x \text{ terms}} = \boxed{\text{numbers}}$$

(Remember to change the sign of any term going across the '=' sign.)

$$-2x + 4 = 3x - 6$$

$$\Rightarrow \quad -2x - 3x = -6 - 4$$

② *Add the terms on each side.*

$$\Rightarrow \quad -5x = -10$$

③ *Evaluate x.*

(Divide the right-hand side by the number before the x term. Because we are **dividing** by the number before the x term its sign does not change.)

$$\Rightarrow \quad x = \frac{-10}{-5}$$

$$\underline{x = +2}$$

Example 2

Solve $-3(2x - 4) + 1 = 2(x + 5)$

① *Multiply out fully.*

$$-3(2x - 4) + 1 = 2(x + 5)$$

$$\Rightarrow \quad -6x + 12 + 1 = 2x + 10$$

② *Rearrange correctly.*

$$\boxed{x \text{ terms}} = \boxed{\text{numbers}}$$

$$-6x + 12 + 1 = 2x + 10$$

$$\Rightarrow \quad -6x - 2x = +10 - 12 - 1$$

③ *Add the terms on each side.*

$$\Rightarrow \quad -8x = -3$$

④ *Solve for x.*

$$x = \frac{-3}{-8} \text{ or } + \frac{3}{8}$$

Example 3 (written problem)

An apple costs 3c more than an orange. 3 apples and 2 oranges cost 94 cents.
Letting x = the cost of an apple, write an equation to represent the information above.
Hence find the cost of an apple.

Solution

'An apple costs 3c more than an orange.'

Cost of apple = x

$\Rightarrow$ Cost of orange = $x - 3$

'3 apples and 2 oranges cost 94 cents

$\Rightarrow 3(x) + 2(x - 3) = 94$

① Multiply out … $3x + 2x - 6 = 94$

② Rearranging … $3x + 2x = 94 + 6$

③ Adding … $5x = 100$

④ Solving for $x \Rightarrow x = \dfrac{100}{5}$

$$\underline{x = 20}$$

Therefore an apple costs 20c.

Example 4

When 3 is taken from a certain number and the result multiplied by 4, the answer is the same as adding 6 to the number. Let the number = x and represent the information above using a single equation. Hence evaluate x.

'3 is taken from a certain number'
$\Rightarrow x - 3$

'the result multiplied by 4' $\Rightarrow$
$4(x - 3)$

'the answer is the same as adding 6 to the number'

$\Rightarrow$ $4(x - 3) = x + 6$

① $4x - 12 = x + 6$

② $4x - 1x = 12 + 6$

③ $3x = 18$

④ $x = \dfrac{18}{3} \Rightarrow \underline{x = 6}$

So, the number is 6.

Section B
Factorising by Grouping

Important

We recognise a 'factorising by grouping' question because:

① It contains four terms.

② It does not have an '=' sign.

Example 1

Factorise $3ax - bx - 3ay + by$

$$3ax - 1bx - 3ay + 1by$$
$$\Downarrow \qquad\qquad \Downarrow$$
$$1x(3a - 1b) - 1y(3a - 1b)$$

We know we are correct because the brackets are the same.

$\Rightarrow$ $(1x - 1y)(3a - 1b)$

Example 2

Factorise $6at + 8af - 9bt - 12bf$

$$2a(3t + 4f) - 3b(3t + 4f)$$

$\Rightarrow$ $\underline{(2a - 3b)(3t + 4f)}$

Section C
Quadratic Equations

A quadratic equation is an equation which contains an x^2 term.

Example 1

Solve $x^2 + 3x - 10 = 0$

Here, two different methods of solving quadratic equations are given. Choose which one you find easier and use that method.

Method 1

$$= (x - 2)(x + 5)$$

> *To check*
>
> $$(x)(x) = x^2 ✓$$
>
> $$(-2)(+5) = -10 ✓$$
>
> $$\overset{-2x}{(x - 2)(x + 5)} \ [+ 5x - 2x = + 3x] ✓$$
>
> $$\underset{+5x}{}$$

$$x - 2 = 0 \qquad x + 5 = 0$$
$$\Rightarrow x = 2 \qquad \Rightarrow x = -5$$

Method 2

> Please read over this method, following each step carefully. After a few examples, it will become very logical.

$$1x^2 + 3x - 10 = 0$$

① Multiply the first and last numbers.

$$(1)(-10) = \underline{-10}$$

② Write down the factors of –10.

$$-10$$
$$\diagup \ \diagdown$$
$$-1 \ + 10$$
$$-2 \ + 5$$

③ Choose the pair of factors which add up to the middle number in the equation (+3).

$$-10$$
$$\diagup \ \diagdown$$
$$-1 \ + 10$$
$$-2 \ + 5 \ ✓$$

④ Substitute '–2x + 5x' into the quadratic equation instead of '+3x'.

$$1x^2 + 3x - 10 = 0$$
$$\Downarrow$$
$$1x^2 - 2x + 5x - 10 = 0$$

⑤ Factorise the equation.

$$1x^2 - 2x + 5x - 10 = 0$$
$$1x(x - 2) + 5(x - 2)$$
$$(1x + 5)(x - 2)$$

⑥ Solve for x.

$$1x + 5 = 0 \qquad x - 2 = 0$$
$$\underline{x = -5} \qquad \underline{x = 2}$$

Example 2

Solve $2x^2 - 7x + 6 = 0$

Method 1

$$(2x - 3)(x - 2)$$

> $$(2x)(x) = 2x^2 ✓$$
>
> $$(-3)(-2) = +6 ✓$$
>
> $$\overset{-3x}{(2x - 3)(x - 2)} \qquad -4x - 3x = -7x ✓$$
>
> $$\underset{-4x}{}$$

$$2x - 3 = 0 \qquad x - 2 = 0$$
$$2x = 3 \qquad \Rightarrow \underline{x = 2}$$
$$\Rightarrow \qquad \underline{x = 3/2}$$

Method 2

① $(2) 6) = \underline{+12}$

② ![+12 branching to factor pairs]

$$
\left.
\begin{array}{l}
-1 \ -12 \\
-2 \ - 6 \\
-3 \ -4
\end{array}
\right\}
$$

- The middle sign is $\ominus$ so the large factors are $\ominus$.
- Factors of $+12$ must have the *same* sign.

③ $-3 \ -4 = -7$
(middle number in eqn.)

④ $$2x^2 - 7x + 6 = 0$$
$$\Downarrow$$
$$2x^2 - 3x - 4x + 6 = 0$$

⑤ $1x(2x - 3) - 2(2x - 3)$
$(1x - 2)(2x - 3)$

⑥ $1x - 2 = 0 \qquad 2x - 3 = 0$
$\Rightarrow \quad \underline{x = 2} \qquad 2x = 3$
$$\Rightarrow \underline{x = 3/2}$$

Example 3

The length of a rectangle is 2 cm longer than its width, as shown. The area of the rectangle is 24 cm².

$x + 2$

x

Write a single equation, in x, to represent the above information and hence solve for x.

$$\text{Length} \times \text{Width} = \text{Area}$$
$$\Rightarrow \qquad (x + 2)(x) = 24$$
$$x^2 + 2x = 24$$

Rearranging correctly

$\boxed{x^2 \text{ term}}\ \boxed{x \text{ term}}\ \boxed{\text{number}} = 0$

Method 1

$$1x^2 + 2x - 24 = 0$$
$$(x + 6)(x - 4)$$

$$(x)(x) = x^2 \checkmark$$
$$(6)(-4) = -24 \checkmark$$

$$
\overset{+6x}{(x + 6)(x - 4)}\ [-4x + 6x = +2x]\checkmark
$$
$$\underset{-4x}{}$$

$$x + 6 = 0 \qquad x - 4 = 0$$
$$\Rightarrow \underline{x = -6} \qquad \Rightarrow \underline{x = 4}$$

x represents a distance and therefore can't be negative.

$$\Rightarrow \underline{x = 4 \text{ cm}}$$

Example 4

Factorise $3x^2 + 7x - 6$

Method 1

$$(3x - 2)(x + 3)$$

$$(3x)(x) = 3x^2 \checkmark$$
$$(-2)(+3) = -6 \checkmark$$

$$
\overset{-2x}{(3x - 2)(x + 3)}\ -2x + 9x = 7x \checkmark
$$
$$\underset{+9x}{}$$

As the question has no '=' sign, we do not leave each bracket equal to 0.

$\Rightarrow \quad 3x^2 + 7x - b = \underline{(3x - 2)(x + 3)}$

Method 2

$$3x^2 + 7x - 6$$
$$(3)(-6) = -18$$

$$\overset{-18}{\diagup\ \diagdown}$$

$-1 + 18$ | Again
$-2 + 9\checkmark$ | • Large Factors must be (+).
$-3 + 6$ | • Factors must have different signs.

$$3x^2 + 7x - 6$$
$$\Downarrow$$
$$3x^2 - 2x + 9x - 6$$
$$1x(3x - 2) + 3(3x - 2)$$
$$\Rightarrow \quad \underline{(1x + 3)(3x - 2)}$$

Section D
Difference of Two Squares

In general

$$(a)^2 - (b)^2$$
$$= (a - b)(a + b)$$

Example 1

Factorise $16x^2 - 25$

As with all questions of this type, we write each term as a squared bracket first.

$$\Rightarrow \quad 16x^2 - 25$$
$$= (4x)^2 - (5)^2$$
$$= \underline{(4x - 5)(4x + 5)}$$

Example 2

Factorise $100a^2d^2 - 36e^2$

$$= (10ad)^2 - (6e)^2$$
$$= \underline{(10ad - 6e)(10ad + 6e)}$$

Example 3

Factorise $49x^2 - 4z^4$

$$= (7x)^2 - (2z^2)^2$$
$$= \underline{(7x - 2z^2)(7x + 2z^2)}$$

Section E
Simultaneous Equations

Important

Before trying to solve simultaneous equations, rearrange each one as follows:

$$\boxed{x \text{ term}}\ \boxed{y \text{ term}} = \boxed{\text{number}}$$

Example 1

Solve for x and y

$$x + 3y + 3 = 0$$
$$2x + 5y + 4 = 0$$
$$\Downarrow$$
$$1x + 3y = -3$$
$$2x + 5y = -4$$

Look at the number in front of each x term.

Multiply the top line by the bottom number.

Multiply the bottom line by the top number.

Make either number (−)

$$\boxed{1}\, x + 3y = -3 \ [\times 2]$$
$$\boxed{2}\, x + 5y = -4 \ [\times -1]$$
$$2x + 6y = -6$$
$$-2x - 5y = 4$$

Adding $\qquad \underline{1y = -2}$

40

Solve for x

Picking *any* equation … $2x + 6y = -6$

$\boxed{y = -2} \Rightarrow 2x + 6(-2) = -6$

$$2x - 12 = -6$$
$$2x = 12 - 6$$
$$2x = 6$$
$$\Rightarrow \underline{x = 3}$$

So $x = 3$ and $y = -2$.

Example 2

In a music shop:

3 tapes and 2 CDs cost €48.

2 tapes and 5 CDs cost €76.

Write two equations, in x and y, to illustrate the above information. Hence, calculate the cost of both a tape and a CD.

> Let x = cost of a tape.
>
> Let y = cost of a CD.

3 tapes and 2 CDs cost €48 …
$3x + 2y = 48$

2 tapes and 5 CDs cost €76 …
$2x + 5y = 76$

Evaluate x and y

$$\boxed{3}\,x + 2y = 48 \ [\times 2]$$
$$\boxed{2}\,x + 5y = 76 \ [\times -3]$$

$$6x + 4y = 96$$
$$-6x - 15y = -228$$
$$\overline{ -11y = -132}$$

$$y = \frac{-132}{-11}$$

$$\Rightarrow \qquad \underline{y = 12}$$

Solve for x

$3x + 2y = 48$

$\boxed{y = 12} \Rightarrow 3x + 2(12) = 48$

$$3x + 24 = 48$$
$$3x = 48 - 24$$
$$3x = 24$$
$$\Rightarrow \qquad \underline{x = 8}$$

Therefore a tape costs €8 and a CD costs €12.

Chapter 4
Sample questions for you to try

Question 1

(a) Solve $2x^2 - 9x + 10 = 0$

(b) *Solve for x and y*

$$3x - 2y = 14$$
$$\underline{2x + 4y = 4}$$

(c) *Solve for x*

$$-3(-2x + 1) + 4x = 2(-4x - 1)$$

(d) Simplify $\dfrac{15tp + 5t^2 - 6fp - 2ft}{25t^2 - 4f^2}$

Question 2

(a) In a newsagent:

2 pens and 3 rulers cost 85c.

3 pens and 4 rulers cost €1.20.

Write two equations, in x and y, to illustrate the above information. Hence, calculate the cost of each item.

(b) Simplify $\dfrac{3x^2 - 4x - 4}{9x^2 - 4}$

(c) *Solve for x*

$$-2(4x - 1) + 2 = 3\,(-2x + 1)$$

Question 3

(a) Factorise each of the following:

   (i) $3ax + 6xb - 2ay - 4by$

   (ii) $4x^2 - 25y^2$

(b) *Solve for a and b*

$$3a + 2b = 16$$
$$\underline{4a - 3b = -7}$$

(c) When twice the square of a number is added to nine times the number, the result is five.

Letting the number $= x$, write a single equation in x, and hence evaluate x.

Solution to question 1

(a) | Solve $2x^2 - 9x + 10 = 0$ |

Method 1

$$(2x - 5)(x - 2)$$

To check
$(2x)(x) = 2x^2\checkmark$
$(-5)(-2) = +10\checkmark$
$(2x - 5)(x - 2) \quad -5x - 4x = -9x\checkmark$ $\overset{-5x}{\frown}$ $\underset{-4x}{\smile}$

$$2x - 5 = 0 \qquad x - 2 = 0$$
$$2x = 5 \qquad\quad \Rightarrow \underline{x = 2}$$
$$\Rightarrow \underline{x = 5/2}$$

Method 2

$$2x^2 - 9x + 10 = 0$$

$(2)(+10) = +20$

$$\begin{array}{c} +20 \\ \diagup\ \diagdown \\ -1 - 20 \\ -2 - 10 \\ -4 - 5\checkmark \end{array}$$

$$2x^2 - 9x + 10 = 0$$
$$\Downarrow$$
$$2x^2 - 4x - 5x + 10 = 0$$
$$2x(x - 2) - 5(x - 2)$$
$$(2x - 5)(x - 2)$$

$$2x - 5 = 0 \qquad x - 2 = 0$$
$$2x = 5 \qquad\quad \Rightarrow \underline{x = 2}$$
$$\Rightarrow \underline{x = 5/2}$$

(b) | Solve for x and y |
| --- |
| $3x - 2y = 14$ |
| $2x + 4y = 4$ |

$$3\,|\,x - 2y = 14 \ [\times 2] \qquad 6x - 4y = 28$$
$$2\,|\,x + 4y = 4 \ [\times -3] \quad \underline{-6x - 12y = -12}$$
$$-16y = 16$$
$$\underline{y = -1}$$

Solve for x

$$3x - 2y = 14$$
$$\boxed{y = -1} \quad 3x - 2(-1) = 14$$
$$3x + 2 = 14$$
$$3x = 14 - 2$$
$$3x = 12 \Rightarrow \underline{x = 4}$$

(c) | Solve $-3(-2x + 1) + 4x = 2(-4x - 1)$ |

$$\Rightarrow \qquad 6x - 3 + 4x = -8x - 2$$

Rearrange … $6x + 4x + 8x = 3 - 2$

$$\Rightarrow 18x = 1$$
$$x = \dfrac{1}{18}$$

(d) Simplify $\dfrac{15tp + 5t^2 - 6fp - 2ft}{25t^2 - 4f^2}$

① $15tp + 5t^2 - 6fp - 2ft$

$\quad = 5t(3p + 1t) - 2f(3p + 1t)$

$\quad (5t - 2f)(3p + 1t)$

② $25t^2 - 4f^2$

$\quad = (5t)^2 - (2f)^2$

$\quad = (5t - 2f)(5t + 2f)$

$\Rightarrow$

$\dfrac{15tp + 5t^2 - 6fp - 2ft}{25t^2 - 4f^2} = \dfrac{(5t-2f)(3p+1t)}{(5t-2f)(5t+2f)}$

$= \dfrac{\cancel{(5t-2f)}(3p+1t)}{\cancel{(5t-2f)}(5t+2f)} = \boxed{\dfrac{3p + 1t}{5t + 2f}}$

Solution to question 2

Let x = cost of a pen.
Let y = cost of a ruler.

(a) '2 pens and 3 rulers cost 85c'

$\underline{2x + 3y = 85}$

'3 pens and 4 rulers cost €1.20'

$\underline{3x + 4y = 120}$

Solve for x and y

$\boxed{2}\,x + 3y = 85\;[\times 3] \qquad 6x + 9y = 255$

$\boxed{3}\,x + 4y = 120\;[\times -2] \quad \underline{-6x - 8y = -240}$

$\qquad\qquad\qquad\qquad\qquad\qquad 1y = 15$

Solve for x

$2x + 3y = 85$

$\boxed{y = 15} \Rightarrow 2x + 3(15) = 85$

$\qquad\qquad 2x + 45 = 85$

$\qquad\qquad 2x = 85 - 45$

$\qquad\qquad 2x = 40$

$\qquad\qquad \Rightarrow \underline{x = 20}$

So a pen costs 20c and a ruler costs 15c.

(b) Simplify $\dfrac{3x^2 - 4x - 4}{9x^2 - 4}$

$= \dfrac{(3x + 2)(x - 2)}{(3x - 2)(3x + 2)}$

$= \dfrac{\cancel{(3x+2)}(x - 2)}{(3x - 2)\cancel{(3x+2)}} = \boxed{\dfrac{x - 2}{3x - 2}}$

(c) Solve $-2(4x - 1) + 2 = 3(-2x + 1)$

$\Rightarrow \qquad -8x + 2 + 2 = -6x + 3$

Rearrange ... $-8x + 6x = 3 - 2 - 2$

$\qquad\qquad -2x = -1$

$\qquad\qquad x = \dfrac{-1}{-2}$

$\Rightarrow$

$\boxed{x = +\dfrac{1}{2}}$

Solution to question 3

(a) (i) Factorise $3ax + 6xb - 2ay - 4by$

$\Rightarrow \qquad 3x(1a + 2b) - 2y(1a + 2b)$

$\qquad\quad = \underline{(3x - 2y)(1a + 2b)}$

(ii) Factorise $4x^2 - 25y^2$

$\qquad = (2x)^2 - (5y)^2$

$\qquad = \underline{(2x - 5y)(2x + 5y)}$

(b) Solve for a and b

$\qquad\qquad 3a + 2b = 16$

$\qquad\qquad 4a - 3b = -7$

$\boxed{3}\,a + 2b = 16\;[\times 4] \qquad 12a + 8b = 64$

$\boxed{4}\,a - 3b = -7\;[\times -3] \quad \underline{-12a + 9b = 21}$

$\qquad\qquad\qquad\qquad\qquad\qquad 17b = 85$

$\qquad\qquad\qquad\qquad\qquad\qquad b = \dfrac{85}{17}$

$\qquad\qquad\qquad\qquad\qquad \Rightarrow \underline{b = 5}$

Solve for a

$3a + 2b = 16$

$\boxed{b = 5}$ $3a + 2(5) = 16$

$$3a + 10 = 16$$

$$3a = 16 - 10$$

$$3a = 6 \Rightarrow \underline{a = 2}$$

(c) | **'Twice the square of a number is added to 9 times the number, the result is 5.'**

Let the number $= x$

$\Rightarrow$ $2x^2 + 9x = 5$

Rearrange ... $2x^2 + 9x - 5 = 0$

Solve for x

$$(2x - 1)(x + 5)$$

$2x - 1 = 0$ $x + 5 = 0$

$2x = 1$ $\Rightarrow \underline{x = -5}$

$\Rightarrow x = \dfrac{1}{2}$

Chapter 5
Fractions and Inequalities

Section A
Fractions

Adding/Subtracting

Example 1

Evaluate $\dfrac{2}{3} + \dfrac{3}{4} - \dfrac{1}{2}$

① Find the LCM of the denominators.

> The denominators (numbers under the line) are 3, 4 and 2.
>
> The smallest number *they all divide into* is 12.

$\Rightarrow$ Lowest Common Multiple = 12

② Rewrite each fraction with 12 as the new denominator.

$$\Rightarrow \quad \overset{\times 4}{\underset{\times 4}{\dfrac{2}{3} = \dfrac{8}{12}}} \qquad \overset{\times 3}{\underset{\times 3}{\dfrac{3}{4} = \dfrac{9}{12}}} \qquad \overset{\times 6}{\underset{\times 6}{\dfrac{1}{2} = \dfrac{6}{12}}}$$

③ Complete the question.

$$\dfrac{8}{12} + \dfrac{9}{12} - \dfrac{6}{12} = \boxed{\dfrac{11}{12}}$$

Example 2

Evaluate $3\dfrac{1}{4} - 2\dfrac{2}{5} + 4\dfrac{3}{10}$

① Add and subtract the whole numbers first.

$$3 - 2 + 4 = 5$$

② Proceed as above.

$$LCM = 20$$

$$\dfrac{1}{4} = \dfrac{5}{20} \qquad \dfrac{2}{5} = \dfrac{8}{20} \qquad \dfrac{3}{10} = \dfrac{6}{20}$$

$$\Rightarrow \qquad \dfrac{5}{20} - \dfrac{8}{20} + \dfrac{6}{20} = \dfrac{3}{20}$$

Therefore $3\dfrac{1}{4} - 2\dfrac{3}{5} + 4\dfrac{3}{10} = \boxed{5\dfrac{3}{20}}$

Multiplication

Example 1

Simplify $\dfrac{3}{4} \times \dfrac{5}{9}$

① Before we start, see if we can divide top and bottom by the same number.

Divide by 3 ... $\dfrac{\overset{1}{3}}{4} \times \dfrac{5}{\underset{3}{9}} \Rightarrow \dfrac{1}{4} \times \dfrac{5}{3}$

② Multiply out

$$\dfrac{1}{4} \times \dfrac{5}{3} = \boxed{\dfrac{5}{12}}$$

Example 2

Simplify $2\frac{5}{8} \times 2\frac{2}{7}$

① Change both into an improper fraction.

$$2\frac{5}{8} = \frac{21}{5} \;[(2 \times 8) + 5]$$

$$2\frac{2}{7} = \frac{16}{7} \;[(2 \times 7) + 2]$$

$$\Rightarrow \qquad \frac{21}{5} \times \frac{16}{7}$$

② Proceed as in Example 1.

$$\frac{21}{5} \times \frac{16}{7}$$

Divide by 7 ... $\dfrac{{}^{3}\cancel{21}}{5} \times \dfrac{16}{\cancel{7}_{1}}$

$$\Rightarrow \qquad \frac{3}{5} \times \frac{16}{1} = \frac{48}{5}$$

$$= \boxed{9\,\frac{3}{5}}$$

Division

Example 1

Simplify $\dfrac{4}{7} \div \dfrac{6}{5}$

Turn the second fraction upside down and multiply.

$$\Rightarrow \qquad \frac{4}{7} \times \frac{5}{6}$$

Divide by 2...

$$\dfrac{{}^{2}\cancel{4}}{7} \times \dfrac{5}{\cancel{6}_{3}} = \frac{2}{7} \times \frac{5}{3} = \boxed{\frac{10}{21}}$$

Example 2

Simplify $6\frac{2}{3} \div 2\frac{4}{9}$

① Change to improper fraction.

$$6\frac{2}{3} \div 2\frac{4}{9} = \frac{20}{3} \div \frac{22}{9}$$

② Turn the second fraction upside down and multiply.

$$\Rightarrow \qquad \frac{20}{3} \times \frac{9}{22}$$

• Divide by 3 ... $\dfrac{20}{\cancel{3}_{1}} \times \dfrac{\cancel{9}^{3}}{22} = \dfrac{20}{1} \times \dfrac{3}{22}$

• Divide by 2 ... $\dfrac{{}^{10}\cancel{20}}{1} \times \dfrac{3}{\cancel{22}_{11}} = \dfrac{10}{1} \times \dfrac{3}{11}$

$$\frac{10}{1} \times \frac{3}{11} = \frac{30}{11} = \boxed{2\,\frac{8}{11}}$$

Section B
Fractions Involving x Terms

Example 1

Simplify $\dfrac{3x - 2}{4} - \dfrac{2x + 1}{3}$

① Find the LCM of the denominators.

LCM of 4 and 3 is 12

② Multiply both fractions by 12.

$$\Rightarrow \qquad \frac{12(3x - 2)}{4} - \frac{12(2x + 1)}{3}$$

$$\Rightarrow \qquad 3(3x - 2) - 4(2x + 1)$$

$\Rightarrow \qquad \dfrac{3(3x-2) - 4(2x+1)}{12}$

③   Multiply out and simplify.

$\Rightarrow \qquad \dfrac{9x - 6 - 8x - 4}{12}$

$\Rightarrow \qquad \boxed{\dfrac{1x - 10}{12}}$

Example 2

Solve $\dfrac{2x-3}{4} - \dfrac{3x+4}{8} = 3$

①   Write *each* term in fraction form.

$\Rightarrow \qquad \dfrac{2x-3}{4} - \dfrac{3x+4}{8} = \dfrac{3}{1}$

②   Find the LCM of the denominators.

$$\underline{LCM = 8}$$

③   Multiply each term by 8.

$\dfrac{8(2x-3)}{4} - \dfrac{8(3x+4)}{8} = \dfrac{8(3)}{1}$

$\Rightarrow \qquad 2(2x-3) - 1(3x+4) = 24$

④   Multiply out and solve.

$$2(2x-3) - 1(3x+4) = 24$$

$\Rightarrow \qquad 4x - 6 - 3x - 4 = 24$

$\qquad\qquad 4x - 3x = 24 + 6 + 4$

$\Rightarrow \qquad\qquad \underline{1x = 34}$

Example 3

(a) Simplify $\dfrac{3x-1}{6} - \dfrac{4x+3}{4}$

(b) Hence solve

$$\dfrac{3x-1}{6} - \dfrac{4x+3}{4} = 2$$

(a) $\boxed{\text{Simplify } \dfrac{3x-1}{6} - \dfrac{4x+3}{4}}$

LCM = 12

$\Rightarrow \qquad \dfrac{12(3x-1)}{6} - \dfrac{12(4x+3)}{4}$

$\Rightarrow \qquad 2(3x-1) - 3(4x+3)$

$\Rightarrow \qquad \dfrac{2(3x-1) - 3(4x+3)}{12}$

$\Rightarrow \qquad \dfrac{6x - 2 - 12x - 9}{12}$

$\Rightarrow \qquad \boxed{\dfrac{-6x - 11}{12}}$

(b) $\boxed{\begin{array}{l} \textit{Hence solve} \\[4pt] \dfrac{3x-1}{6} - \dfrac{4x+3}{4} = 2 \end{array}}$

Substitute our answer for part (a) into this question … We found

$\dfrac{3x-1}{6} - \dfrac{4x+3}{4}$ is $\dfrac{-6x-11}{12}$

Solve $\dfrac{3x-1}{6} - \dfrac{4x+3}{4} = 2$

$\Downarrow$

Solve $\dfrac{-6x-11}{12} = 2$

Solve $\dfrac{-6x-11}{12} = 2$

① Write both terms as fractions.

$\Rightarrow \qquad \dfrac{-6x-11}{12} = \dfrac{2}{1}$

② LCM = 12

③ $\Rightarrow \qquad \dfrac{12(-6x-11)}{12} = \dfrac{12(2)}{1}$

$\Rightarrow \qquad 1(-6x - 11) = 24$

Solving $\qquad -6x - 11 = 24$

$\Rightarrow \qquad\qquad -6x = 24 + 11$

$\qquad\qquad\qquad -6x = 35$

$\Rightarrow \qquad\qquad x = \dfrac{35}{-6}$

$\Rightarrow \qquad\qquad x = -5\dfrac{5}{6}$

Section C
Inequalities

Graphing inequalities

① Natural numbers [N]

Graph $x < 4$, $x \in N$

> *Natural numbers*
> - are positive.
> - are whole numbers only.

$x < 4$ 'x less than 4'

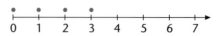

We do not include 4 as x is not equal to 4.

② Integers [Z]

Graph $x \geqslant -2$, $x \in Z$

> *Integers*
> - are positive *and* negative.
> - are whole numbers only.

$x \geqslant -2$ 'x greater than or equal to -2'

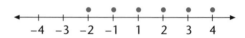

We include -2 as x *is* equal to -2.

③ Real numbers [R]

> *Real numbers*
> - are positive and negative.
> - include all whole numbers, fractions and decimals.
> - are shown on the number line using a shaded line.

Example 1

Graph $x \leqslant 2\dfrac{1}{2}$, $x \in R$

$2^{1}/_{2}$

Example 2

Graph $x > -1.2$, $x \in R$

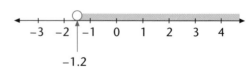

-1.2

Solving inequalities

Inequalities are solved in exactly the same way as normal equations except:

Important

When the x term is negative we must:

① Change the sign on both sides of the inequality.

② Change the direction of the inequality.

Example

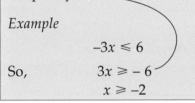

$$-3x \leqslant 6$$

So, $$3x \geqslant -6$$

$$x \geqslant -2$$

Example 1

Solve $2(x + 1) \leqslant 10$, $x \in N$ and graph on the appropriate number line.

$$2(x + 1) \leqslant 10$$

$$2x + 2 \leqslant 10$$

$$\Rightarrow \qquad 2x \leqslant 10 - 2$$

$$2x \leqslant 8$$

$$\boxed{x \leqslant 4}$$

(Natural numbers)

Example 2

Solve $3(2x - 1) < 8x + 1$, $x \in Z$ and graph on the appropriate number line.

$$3(2x - 1) < 8x + 1$$

$$\Rightarrow \qquad 6x - 3 < 8x + 1$$

Rearranging

$$6x - 8x < 1 + 3$$

$$-2x < 4$$

Here the x term is (–) so we:

① Change both signs. ② Change the direction of the inequality.

$$-2x < 4$$

$$\Rightarrow \qquad 2x > -4$$

So, $$\boxed{x > -2}$$

(Integers)

Example 3

Solve $-3(2x + 1) \geqslant -2(x - 3)$, $x \in R$ and illustrate on the number line.

$$-3(2x + 1) \geqslant -2(x - 3)$$

$$\Rightarrow \qquad -6x - 3 \geqslant -2x + 6$$

$$-6x + 2x \geqslant 6 + 3$$

$$-4x \geqslant 9$$

Again, the x term here is negative.

$$\Rightarrow \qquad 4x \leqslant -9$$

$$x \leqslant -\frac{9}{4}$$

$$\boxed{x \leqslant -2\frac{1}{4}}$$

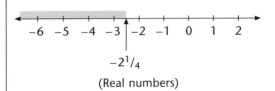

$-2^1/_4$

(Real numbers)

Section D
Multiplication Involving x Terms

Example 1

Multiply $2x^2 - 3x + 1$ by $2x - 1$

① **Write both terms in brackets.**

$$(2x - 1)(2x^2 - 3x + 1)$$

② **'Break up' the smaller term and multiply each part by the larger term.**

$$\underline{(2x - 1)}(2x^2 - 3x + 1)$$

$$\underline{2x}(2x^2 - 3x + 1) \underline{-1}(2x^2 - 3x + 1)$$

$$4x^3 - 6x^2 + 2x - 2x^2 + 3x - 1$$

③ Simplify by rearranging and then adding similar terms.

$$4x^3 - 6x^2 - 2x^2 + 2x + 3x - 1$$

$$\underline{4x^3 - 8x^2 + 5x - 1}$$

Example 2

Multiply $3x^2 - 2x - 1$ by $2x + 3$

① $\underline{(2x + 3)}(3x^2 - 2x - 1)$

② $\underline{2x}(3x^2 - 2x - 1) \underline{+ 3}(3x^2 - 2x - 1)$

$$6x^3 - 4x^2 - 2x + 9x^2 - 6x - 3$$

③ $6x^3 - 4x^2 + 9x^2 - 2x - 6x - 3$

$$= \underline{6x^3 + 5x^2 - 8x - 3}$$

Chapter 5
Sample questions for you to try

Question 1

(a) Solve $2(2x - 1) < 6(x + 1)$, $x \in Z$

and illustrate on the appropriate number line.

(b) Simplify $\dfrac{3x - 2}{3} - \dfrac{2x - 5}{6}$

(c) Multiply $2x^2 - 4x - 3$ by $3x + 2$

(d) Evaluate $2.4 + 3.5 \times 2.9$ correct to one decimal place.

Question 2

(a) Multiply $4x^2 - 2x + 3$ by $2x + 1$

(b) Solve $3(-2x + 1) \geqslant -2x - 5$, $x \in N$ and illustrate on the appropriate number line.

(c) Solve $\dfrac{4x - 3}{2} - \dfrac{5x + 1}{6} = 3$

Question 3

(a) (i) Simplify $\dfrac{2x - 5}{8} - \dfrac{3x - 2}{4}$

   (ii) Hence, or otherwise, solve

$$\dfrac{2x - 5}{8} - \dfrac{3x - 2}{4} = 2$$

(b) Evaluate

   (i) $2\dfrac{2}{3} \times \dfrac{9}{16}$

   (ii) $5\dfrac{5}{8} \div 6\dfrac{1}{4}$

(c) Evaluate

   (i) $5.2 - 3.2 \div 6.1$

   (ii) $3.12 + 2.6 \times 3.21$

giving your answer correct to two decimal places in both cases.

Solution to question 1

(a) | Solve and graph
$$2(2x-1) < 6(x+1), x \in Z$$

$\Rightarrow$ $\qquad 4x - 2 < 6x + 6$

$\qquad\qquad 4x - 6x < 6 + 2$

$\qquad\qquad -2x < 8$

The x term is negative $\Rightarrow 2x > -8$

$$\boxed{x > -4}$$

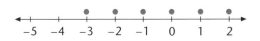

-5   -4   -3   -2   -1   0   1   2

(b) | Simplify $\dfrac{3x-2}{3} - \dfrac{2x-5}{6}$

$\boxed{\text{LCM} = 6}$

$$\frac{6(3x-2)}{3} - \frac{6(2x-5)}{6}$$

$$\frac{2(3x-2) - 1(2x+5)}{6}$$

$$\frac{6x - 4 - 2x + 5}{6} \Rightarrow \boxed{\frac{4x+1}{6}}$$

(c) | Multiply $2x^2 - 4x - 3$ by $3x + 2$

$\Rightarrow \qquad (3x+2)(2x^2 - 4x - 3)$

$\qquad \underline{3x}(2x^2 - 4x - 3) \underline{+ 2}(2x^2 - 4x - 3)$

$\qquad 6x^3 - 12x^2 - 9x + 4x^2 - 8x - 6$

$\Rightarrow \quad 6x^3 - 12x^2 + 4x^2 - 9x - 8x - 6$

$\qquad = \underline{6x^3 - 8x^2 - 17x - 6}$

(d) | Evaluate $2.4 + 3.5 \times 2.9$ correct to 1 decimal place.

$$2.4 + 3.5 \times 2.9 = \underline{12.55}$$

To express 'correct to 1 dec. place'.

① Look at the *second* decimal place.

② If this is greater than or equal to 5, increase the first decimal place by one.

$\Rightarrow \qquad 2.4 + 3.5 \times 2.9 = \underline{12.6}$

Solution to question 2

(a) | Multiply $4x^2 - 2x + 3$ by $2x + 1$

$$\underline{(2x+1)}(4x^2 - 2x + 3)$$

$$\underline{2x}(4x^2 - 2x + 3) \underline{+ 1}(4x^2 - 2x + 3)$$

$$= 8x^3 - 4x^2 + 6x + 4x^2 - 2x + 3$$

$$= 8x^3 - 4x^2 + 4x^2 + 6x - 2x + 3$$

$$= \underline{8x^3 + 4x + 3}$$

(b) | Solve and graph
$$3(-2x+1) \geqslant -2x - 5, x \in N$$

$\Rightarrow \qquad -6x + 3 \geqslant -2x - 5$

$\Rightarrow \qquad -6x + 2x \geqslant -3 - 5$

$\Rightarrow \qquad -4x \geqslant -8$

Again we notice the x term is negative.

$\Rightarrow \qquad\qquad 4x \leqslant 8$

$$\boxed{x \leqslant 2}$$

0   1   2   3   4   5   6

(c) Solve $\dfrac{4x-3}{2} - \dfrac{5x+1}{6} = 3$

$$\frac{4x-3}{2} - \frac{5x+1}{6} = \frac{3}{1}$$

$\boxed{\text{LCM} = 6}$

$$\frac{6(4x-3)}{2} - \frac{6(5x+1)}{6} = \frac{6(3)}{1}$$

51

$$\Rightarrow \quad 3(4x - 3) - 1(5x + 1) = 6(3)$$
$$12x - 9 - 5x - 1 = 18$$
$$\Rightarrow \quad 12x - 5x = 18 + 9 + 1$$
$$7x = 28$$
$$\Rightarrow \quad x = \frac{28}{7} \quad \boxed{x = 4}$$

Solution to question 3

(a) (i) Simplify $\dfrac{2x - 5}{8} - \dfrac{3x - 2}{4}$

LCM = 8

$$\Rightarrow \quad \frac{8(2x - 5)}{8} - \frac{8(3x - 2)}{4}$$

$$\Rightarrow \quad \frac{1(2x - 5) - 2(3x - 2)}{8}$$

$$\Rightarrow \quad \frac{2x - 5 - 6x + 4}{8} = \boxed{\frac{-4x - 1}{8}}$$

(ii) Hence, or otherwise, solve

$$\frac{2x - 5}{8} - \frac{3x - 2}{4} = 2$$

$$\frac{2x - 5}{8} - \frac{3x - 2}{4} = 2$$

$$\Rightarrow \quad \frac{-4x - 1}{8} = 2$$

$$\Rightarrow \quad \frac{-4x - 1}{8} = \frac{2}{1}$$

LCM = 8

$$\frac{8(-4x - 1)}{8} = \frac{8(2)}{1}$$

$$\Rightarrow \quad 1(-4x - 1) = 8(2)$$
$$-4x - 1 = 16$$
$$-4x = 16 + 1$$
$$-4x = 17$$

$$\Rightarrow \quad x = \frac{17}{-4}$$

(b) (i) Evaluate $2\dfrac{2}{3} \times \dfrac{9}{16}$

$$\Rightarrow \quad \frac{8}{3} \times \frac{9}{16}$$

$$[\div 3] \Rightarrow \frac{8}{{}_1\cancel{3}} \times \frac{\cancel{9}^3}{16} = \frac{8}{1} \times \frac{3}{16}$$

$$[\div 8] \Rightarrow \frac{\cancel{8}^1}{1} \times \frac{3}{{}_2\cancel{16}} = \frac{1}{1} \times \frac{3}{2}$$

$$= \boxed{\frac{3}{2}}$$

(ii) Evaluate $5\dfrac{5}{8} \div 6\dfrac{1}{4}$

$$= \frac{45}{8} \div \frac{25}{4}$$

$$= \frac{45}{8} \times \frac{4}{25}$$

$$[\div 4] \quad \frac{45}{{}_2\cancel{8}} \times \frac{\cancel{4}^1}{25} = \frac{45}{2} \times \frac{1}{25}$$

$$[\div 5] \quad \frac{\cancel{45}^9}{2} \times \frac{1}{{}_5\cancel{25}} = \frac{9}{2} \times \frac{1}{5}$$

$$= \boxed{\frac{9}{10}}$$

(c) (i) Evaluate 5.2 − 3.2 ÷ 6.1 correct to two decimal places.

$$5.2 - 3.2 \div 6.1 = 4.675$$
$$= \underline{4.68}$$

The third decimal place is 5 so the second decimal place increases by one.

(ii) Evaluate 3.12 + 2.6 × 3.2 correct to 2 decimal places.

$$3.12 + 2.6 \times 3.2 = 11.466$$
$$= \underline{11.47}$$

Chapter 6
Functions and Graphs

Section A
Functions, Domain/Range

Functions

In general

Given the function

$$f: x \rightarrow 3x^2 - 2x + 1$$

we find $f(a)$ by substituting (a) into the function instead of the x term.

$$\Rightarrow \quad f(a) = 3(a)^2 - 2(a) + 1$$
$$= \underline{3a^2 - 2a + 1}$$
$$f(-2) = 3(-2)^2 - 2(-2) + 1$$
$$= 3(4) - 2(-2) + 1$$
$$= 12 + 4 + 1 = \underline{17}$$

Type 1

Given the function

$$f: x \rightarrow 4x - 1$$

Evaluate:

(i) $f(-6)$

(ii) $f(3t + 1)$

(iii) Solve for $f(5a - 2) = 11$

(i) *f(–6)*

$$f: x \rightarrow 4x - 1$$
$$\Rightarrow \quad f(-6) = 4(-6) - 1$$
$$= -24 - 1 = \underline{-25}$$

(ii) *f(3t + 1)*

$$f: x \rightarrow 4x - 1$$
$$\Rightarrow \quad f(3t + 1) = 4(3t + 1) - 1$$
$$= 12t + 4 - 1 = \underline{12t + 3}$$

(iii) *Solve for f(5a – 2) = 11*

① *Find $f(5a - 2)$*

$$f: x \rightarrow 4x - 1$$
$$\Rightarrow \quad f(5a - 2) = 4(5a - 2) - 1$$
$$= 20a - 8 - 1 = \underline{20a - 9}$$

② *Solve for a*

$$f(5a - 2) = 11$$
$$\Rightarrow \qquad 20a - 9 = 11$$
$$20a = 11 + 9$$
$$20a = 20 \quad \Rightarrow \underline{a = 1}$$

Type 2

Given the function

$$g: x \rightarrow 2x^2 - 3x + 1$$

Evaluate:

(i) $g(-3)$

(ii) $g(2n)$

(iii) $g(3p)$

(iv) Solve for $g(t) = 0$

(i) *g(–3)*

$$g: x \rightarrow 2x^2 - 3x + 1$$
$$\Rightarrow \quad g(-3) = 2(-3)^2 - 3(-3) + 1$$

Important

When evaluating $2(-3)^2$:

Type $\boxed{2 \; (\pm \; 3) \; x^2}$

$$= 18$$

$$\Rightarrow \quad g(-3) = 18 + 9 + 1$$
$$= \underline{28}$$

(ii) *g(2n)*

$$g: x \rightarrow 2x^2 - 3x + 1$$
$$\Rightarrow \quad g(2n) = 2(2n)^2 - 3(2n) + 1$$

Important

When evaluating $2(2n)^2$:

① Find $(2n)^2$ *first.*

Remember to square both the number *and* the letter.

$$\Rightarrow \quad (2n)^2 = 4n^2$$

② Multiply your answer by 2.

$$\Rightarrow \quad 2(2n)^2 = 2(4n^2) = \underline{8n^2}$$

$$\Rightarrow \quad g(2n) = \underline{8n^2 - 6n + 1}$$

(iii) *g(3p)*

$$g: x \rightarrow 2x^2 - 3x + 1$$
$$\Rightarrow \quad g(3p) = 2(3p)^2 - 3(3p) + 1$$
$$= 2(9p^2) - 3(3p) + 1$$
$$= \underline{18p^2 - 9p + 1}$$

(iv) *Solve for g(t) = 0*

① *Evaluate g(t)*

$$g: x \rightarrow 2x^2 - 3x + 1$$
$$\Rightarrow \quad g(t) = 2t^2 - 3t + 1$$

② Solve for *t*

$$g(t) = 0$$
$$\Rightarrow \quad 2t^2 - 3t + 1 = 0$$

We solve as we would any quadratic equation.

$$2t^2 - 3t + 1 = 0$$

$$(2)(1) = 2$$

$$\begin{array}{c} 2 \\ \diagdown \diagup \diagdown \\ -1 \; -2 \end{array}$$

$$\Rightarrow \quad 2t^2 - 1t - 2t + 1$$
$$1t(2t - 1) - 1(2t - 1)$$
$$(1t - 1)(2t - 1)$$

$1t - 1 = 0$	$2t - 1 = 0$
$\underline{1t = 1}$	$2t = 1$
	$\underline{t = {}^1/_2}$

Domain/Range

Type 1

Given the couples (3 – 4)

(2, 7) and (–4, –3) list the domain and range.

Domain (first term of each couple)

$$= \{3, 2, -4\}$$

Range (second term of each couple)

$$= \{-4, 7, -3\}$$

Please note that the domain and range lists must always be written in chain brackets as shown.

Type 2

$$f: x \rightarrow 2x^2 - 4x$$

The domain of $f(x)$ is {–3, 2, 4}. Find the range of $f(x)$.

Important

To find the range of $f(x)$, simply substitute each domain value in for x in the given equation.

$$f: x \rightarrow 2x^2 - 4x$$
$$f(-3) = 2(-3)^2 - 4(-3)$$
$$= 2(9) + 12 = \underline{30}$$
$$f(2) = 2(2)^2 - 4(2)$$
$$= 2(4) - 8 = \underline{0}$$
$$f(4) = 2(4)^2 - 4(4)$$
$$= 2(16) - 16 = \underline{16}$$

Therefore the range of $f(x)$ is $\{30, 0, 16\}$.

Section B
Graphing Lines

Type 1

Graph the lines $x - y + 5 = 0$ and $2x + y + 2 = 0$ on the same graph, in the domain $-3 \leqslant x \leqslant 1$.

①   *Graph $x - y + 5 = 0$*

x	$x - y + 5 = 0$	y
-3	$(-3) - y + 5 = 0$ $\Rightarrow -y + 2 = 0$	2
-2	$-2 - y + 5 = 0$ $\Rightarrow -y + 3 = 0$	3
-1	$-1 - y + 5 = 0$ $\Rightarrow -y + 4 = 0$	4
0	$0 - y + 5 = 0$ $\Rightarrow -y + 5 = 0$	5
1	$1 - y + 5 = 0$ $\Rightarrow -y + 6 = 0$	6

$\Rightarrow$ $(-3, 2), (-2, 3), (-1, 4), (0, 5)$ and $(1, 6)$

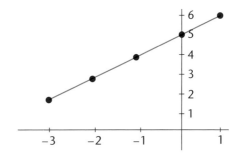

②   *Graph $2x + y + 2 = 0$*

x	$2x + y + 2 = 0$	y
-3	$2(-3) + y + 2 = 0$ $\Rightarrow -6 + y + 2 = 0$ $\Rightarrow y - 4 = 0$	4
-2	$2(-2) + y + 2 = 0$ $-4 + y + 2 = 0$ $y - 2 = 0$	2
-1	$2(-1) + y + 2 = 0$ $-2 + y + 2 = 0$ $y + 0 = 0$	0
0	$2(0) + y + 2 = 0$ $\Rightarrow y + 2 = 0$	-2
1	$2(1) + y + 2 = 0$ $2 + y + 2 = 0$ $\Rightarrow y + 4 = 0$	-4

$\Rightarrow$ $(-3, 4)(-2, 2)(-1, 0)(0, -2)$ and $(1, -4)$

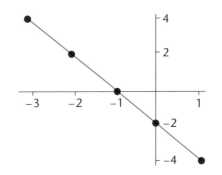

③ **Graph the lines on the same diagram.**

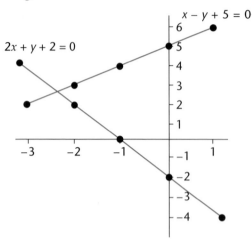

2x + y + 2 = 0

x − y + 5 = 0

Type 2

Given the lines $x + y - 3 = 0$ and $2x + y - 4 = 0$

(i) Graph the lines on the same diagram. Hence estimate the point of intersection.

(ii) Verify your answer by solving for x and y.

$$x + y - 3 = 0$$
$$2x + y - 4 = 0$$

(i) Graph $x + y - 3 = 0$ and $2x + y - 4 = 0$

$$\underline{x + y - 3 = 0}$$

Important

We are not told which values of x to fill in. Therefore, to draw this line we let $x = 0$ and $y = 0$.

$$\underline{x + y - 3 = 0}$$

$\underline{x = 0} \Rightarrow y - 3 = 0 \Rightarrow y = 3$

$\underline{y = 0} \Rightarrow x - 3 = 0 \Rightarrow x = 3$

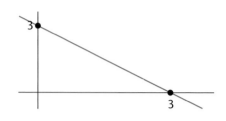

$$2x + y - 4 = 0$$

$\underline{x = 0} \Rightarrow 2(0) + y - 4 = 0 \Rightarrow y = 4$

$\underline{y = 0} \Rightarrow 2x + 0 - 4 = 0 \Rightarrow 2x = 4$

$$x = 2$$

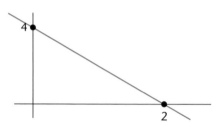

Graph the lines together.

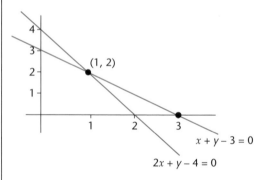

$$x + y - 3 = 0$$
$$2x + y - 4 = 0$$

As we can see from the diagram, the point of intersection may be estimated to be (1, 2).

(ii) Verify the point of intersection by solving:

$$x + y - 3 = 0$$
$$2x + y - 4 = 0$$

$x + y - 3 = 0 \Rightarrow x + y = 3 \; [x - 2]$

$2x + y - 4 = 0 \qquad 2x + y = 4$

$$-2x - 2y = -6$$
$$\underline{2x + 1y = 4}$$
$$-1y = -2 \quad \Rightarrow \quad \boxed{y = 2}$$

$$\underline{x + y = 3}$$

$$y = 2 \quad \Rightarrow \quad x + 2 = 3 \quad \Rightarrow \quad \boxed{x = 1}$$

Therefore the point of intersection is verified as (1, 2).

Section C
Graphing Quadratic Graphs

Type 1

Draw the graph of $f: x \to 2x^2 + x - 3$ in the domain $-2 \leqslant x \leqslant 2$.

From the graph find:

(i) The values for which $f(x) = 0$.

(ii) The values for which $f(x) = 2\frac{1}{2}$.

(iii) The values for which
$$2x^2 + x - 3 = -1.$$

(iv) The value of $f(-0.8)$.

(v) The value of $f(0)$.

(vi) The minimum value of $f(x)$.

(vii) The minimum coordinate.

(a) Complete the table for the graph

x	-2	-1	0	1	2	
$2x^2$						①
$+1x$						②
-3						③
y						

Notes on making out the table

Row ①

We fill all the given x values into $2x^2$ as follows:

$2(-2)^2$ Again we type 2 (⊞ 2) x^2 = 8

$2(-1)^2$ 2(⊞ 1) x^2 = 2

$2(0)^2$ 2(0) x^2 = 0

$2(1)^2$ 2(1) x^2 = 2

$2(2)^2$ 2(2) x^2 = 8

*All the answers in the x^2 row will have the same sign.

Row ②

We fill all the given x values into $+1x$ as follows:

$+1 (-2)$ 1 (⊞ 2)   = -2

$+1 (-1)$ 1 (⊞ 1)   = -1

$+1 (0)$ 1 (0)   = 0

$+1 (1)$ 1 (1)   = 1

$+1 (2)$ 1 (2)   = 2

Row ③

Because the term does not contain an x term or an x^2 term we simply write -3 all the way across.

x	-2	-1	0	1	2
$2x^2$	8	2	0	2	8
$+1x$	-2	-1	0	1	2
-3	-3	-3	-3	-3	-3
y	3	-2	-3	0	7

The points on the graph then are:

(-2, 3) (-1, -2) (0, -3) (1, 0) (2, 7)

Notes on drawing the graph

The x-axis

① The *x* values are from –2 to +2 so make these values the start and finish of the *x*-axis if you can.

② Use the full width of the page for the *x*-axis.

③ Make sure the *x* values are spaced out equally.

The y-axis

① Please ensure that the *y* values are spaced out equally.

② The space between the *y* values does *not* have to be the same as the space between the *x* values.

Sketching the graph

① Always use a pencil to sketch the graph (never a pen).

② The graph must be drawn freehand (not with a ruler).

Points (–2, 3) (–1, –2) (0, –3) (1, 0) (2, 7)

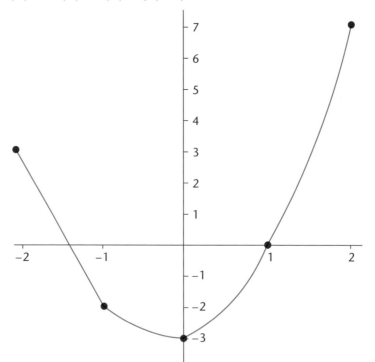

Questions from the Quadratic Graph

Type 1

'Solve for $f(x) = a$'

• $f(x)$ means 'y'

• Therefore, go to the value 'a' on the *y*-axis.

• Find the corresponding *x* value(s).

(i) Solve for $f(x) = 0$

• Go to 0 on the *y*-axis.

• Find the corresponding *x* value(s).

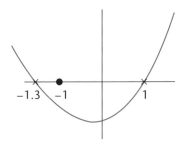

$\Rightarrow$ $\boxed{x = -1.3 \text{ and } x = 1}$

These are the values at which the graph cuts the x-axis.

(ii) *Solve for f(x) = $2^{1}/_{2}$*

- Go to $2\,^{1}/_{2}$ on the y-axis.
- Find the corresponding x value(s).

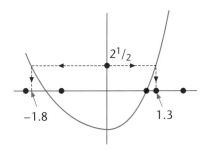

$\boxed{x = -1.8 \text{ and } x = 1.3}$

Note

① **Mark the answers onto the graph.**

② **When giving an answer, always state whether it's the x or y value.**

Type 2

'Solve for Equation = a' of the graph.

- Equation of the graph means y.
- Therefore go to the value 'a' on the y-axis.
- Find the corresponding x value(s).

(iii) *Find the values for which $2x^2 + x - 3 = -1$*

- So 'Equation of the graph' = -1
  $\Rightarrow \quad y = -1$
- Go to -1 on the y-axis.
- Find the corresponding x values.

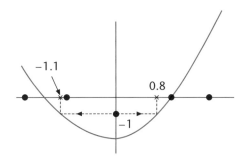

$\Rightarrow$ $\boxed{x = -1.1 \text{ and } x = 0.8}$

Type 3

'Find the value of $f(a)$.'

- Because the value 'a' is inside the bracket, we go to that value on the x-axis.
- Find the corresponding y value.
  (There can only be one.)

(iv) *Find the value of $f(-0.8)$*

- Go to -0.8 on the x-axis.
- Find the corresponding y value.

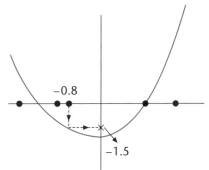

59

$\Rightarrow$ $\boxed{y = -1.5}$

(v) *Find the value of f(0)*

- Go to 0 on the *x*-axis.
- Find the corresponding *y* value.

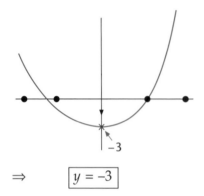

$\Rightarrow$ $\boxed{y = -3}$

Type 4

> 'The minimum value of *f(x)*' and
> 'The minimum coordinate'

Minimum value of f(x)

- Go to the lowest point of the graph.
- Give the *y* value corresponding to this point.

Minimum coordinate

- Go to the lowest point of the graph.
- Give both *x* and *y* values.

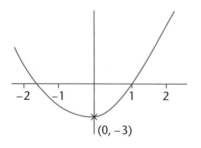

(vi) Minimum value of *f(x)* is – 3

(vii) Minimum coordinate is (0, 3)

Please note that if the graph was ∩ shaped, we could be asked the *maximum* value of *f(x)*.

Simply go to the *highest* point on the graph.

Final Type

(not asked in this example)

> 'The equation of the axis of symmetry.'

- Draw a vertical line through the lowest/highest point of the graph.
- Look at where the line cuts the *x*-axis.
- If it cuts at *x* = 4, the equation of the axis of symmetry is '*x* = 4'.

Section D
Stories and Problem-solving Involving the Quadratic Graph

Example

Graph the function *f*: $x \rightarrow -2x^2 + 2x + 11$ in the domain $-2 \leqslant x \leqslant 3$.

Let the graph represent the flight of a missile fired 1 metre below ground level.

The *x*-axis represents time with *x* = –2 representing 10 a.m., *x* = –1 representing 11 a.m. etc.

The *y*-axis represents the height of the missile with the gap between each *x* value being 1 metre.

Use the graph to find:

(i) The height of the missile at 1.30 p.m.

(ii) At what times was the missile at ground level?

(iii) At what times was the missile 4 metres above the ground?

(iv) What was the maximum height reached by the missile?

(v) At what time was the maximum height reached?

Graph *f*: $x \rightarrow -2x^2 + 2x + 11$ in the domain $-2 \leqslant x \leqslant 3$

① *Complete the table.*

x	-2	-1	0	1	2	3	
$-2x^2$	-8	-2	0	-2	-8	-18	*
$+2x$	-4	-2	0	2	4	6	
$+11$	11	11	11	11	11	11	
y	-1	7	11	11	7	-1	

Points $(-2, -1)$ $(-1, 7)$ $(0, 11)$ $(1, 11)$ $(2, 7)$ $(3, -1)$

*Note on completing row **

We fill the given *x* values into $-2x^2$ as follows:

$$-2(-2)^2 \boxed{\pm}\ 2\ (\boxed{\pm}\ 2)\ \boxed{x^2} = -8 \text{ etc.}$$

② *Draw the graph.*

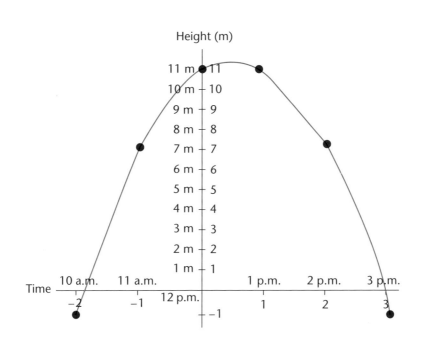

Questions on the graph

(i)   The height of the missile at 1.30 p.m.

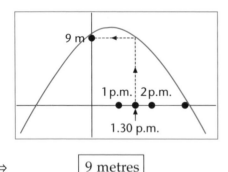

$\Rightarrow$ 9 metres

(ii)   At what times was the missile at ground level?

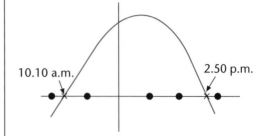

$\Rightarrow$ At 2.50 p.m. and 10.10 a.m.

(iii) At what times was the missile 4 metres above the ground?

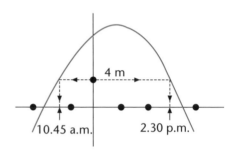

$\Rightarrow$ At 10.45 a.m. and 2.30 p.m.

(iv) What was the maximum height reached by the missile?

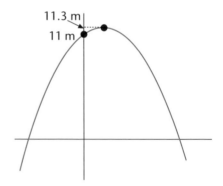

Important

Please understand that giving an answer of 11 m here is wrong.

The graph clearly 'goes up' higher than 11 between the two points shown.

⇒ 11.3 metres

(v) At what time did the missile reach maximum height?

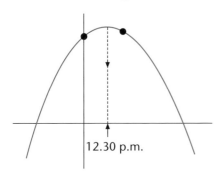

12.30 p.m.

• Go to exactly halfway between the two points shown.

⇒ 12.30 p.m.

Question 1

(a) Given the function $f: x \rightarrow 3x - 5$

    (i) Evaluate $f(-2)$.

    (ii) Evaluate $f(4t)$.

    (iii) Solve for $f(2a) = 1$.

(b) Draw the graph of $f: x \rightarrow 2x^2 - 2x - 3$ in the domain $-2 \leqslant x \leqslant 3$.

Use the graph to find:

    (i) The values for which $f(x) = 0$.

    (ii) The values for which $f(x) = 3$.

    (iii) The value corresponding to $f(1^1/_2)$.

    (iv) The minimum coordinate.

    (v) The equation of the axis of symmetry.

Question 2

(a) (i) List the domain and range of the following couples $(2, -1)$, $(-1, 4)$, $(0, 6)$ and $(-3, -5)$.

(ii) $h: x \rightarrow 2x^2 - 3$. The domain of $h(x)$ is $\{-3, -2, -1, 0, 1, 2\}$. Find the range of $h(x)$.

(b) Graph $f: x \rightarrow -x^2 - 2x + 3$ in the domain $-4 \leqslant x \leqslant 2$.

From the graph:

(i) Solve for $f(x) = 1$.

(ii) Solve for $-x^2 - 2x + 3 = -3$.

(iii) Solve for $f(-1.5)$.

(iv) Solve for $f(0)$.

(v) Find the maximum value of $f(x)$.

Solution to question 1

(a) $f: x \rightarrow 3x - 5$

    (i) *Evaluate f(–2)*

$$f(x) = 3x - 5$$
$$\Rightarrow \quad f(-2) = 3(-2) - 5$$
$$f(-2) = -6 - 5$$

So $\underline{f(-2) = -11}$

    (ii) *Evaluate f(4t)*

$$f(x) = 3x - 5$$
$$\Rightarrow \quad f(4t) = 3(4t) - 5$$

So $\underline{f(4t) = 12t - 5}$

    (iii) *Solve for f(2a) = 1*

$$f(x) = 3x - 5$$
$$f(2a) = 3(2a) - 5$$
$$= 6a - 5$$

Solve for a

$$6a - 5 = 1$$

$$6a = 6$$

$$\underline{a = 1}$$

(b) Complete the table

x	−2	−1	0	1	2	3
$2x^2$	8	2	0	2	8	18
$-2x$	4	2	0	−2	−4	−6
-3	−3	−3	−3	−3	−3	−3
y	9	1	−3	−3	1	9

The points of the graph are:

$(-2, 9)(-1, 1)(0, -3)(1, -3)(2, 1)(3, 9)$

(i) ***The values for which f(x) = 0.***

'*f(x)*' means '*y*' ($\Rightarrow y = 0$)

- So go to 0 on the *y*-axis.
- Find the corresponding *x* values.

> * Again, these are the points where the graph cuts the *x*-axis.

$\Rightarrow \underline{x = -0.8}$ and $\underline{x = 1.8}$

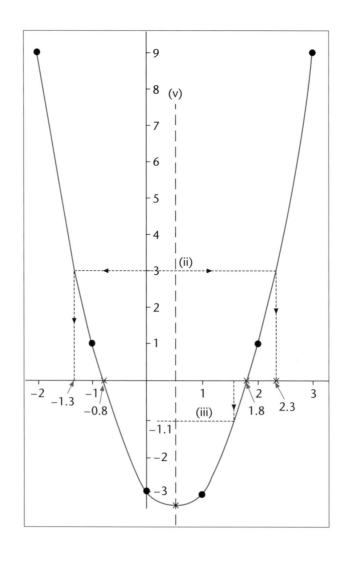

(ii) *The values for which f(x) = 3.*

- Go to 3 on the *y*-axis.
- Find the corresponding *x* values.

  $\Rightarrow$ *x* = −1.3 and *x* = 2.3

* This is indicated by line (ii).

(iii) *The value corresponding to f(1^1/$_2$).*

- Go to 1^1/$_2$ on the *x*-axis.
- Find the corresponding *y* value.

  $\Rightarrow$ *y* = −1.1

* This is indicated by the line (iii).

(iv) *The minimum coordinate.*

This is the lowest point on the graph.

  $\Rightarrow$ (0.5, −3.3)

(v) *The equation of the axis of symmetry.*

- Draw the vertical line through the lowest point.
- It cuts the *x*-axis at *x* = ^{1}/$_2$.

  $\Rightarrow$ Equation of the axis of symmetry is X = ^{1}/$_2$.

* The vertical line is marked (v).

Solution to question 2

(a) **(i) List the domain and range of (2, −1)(−1, 4)(0, 6)(−3, −5).**

- The domain of each couple is the *first* value

  $\Rightarrow$ {2, −1, 0, −3}

- The range of each couple is the *second* value

  = {−1, 4, 6, −5}

(ii) *h*: *x* $\rightarrow$ 2*x*^{2} − 3

The domain of *h*(*x*) is {−3, −2, −1, 0, 1, 2}

Find the range of *h*(*x*).

$h(x) = 2x^2 - 3$

$x = -3$ $h(-3) = 2(-3)^2 - 3$
$= 2(9) - 3 = ⑮$

$x = -2$ $h(2) = 2(2)^2 - 3$
$= 2(4) - 3 = ⑤$

$x = -1$ $h(1) = 2(1)^2 - 3$
$= 2(1) - 3 = Ⓐ$

$x = 0$ $h(0) = 2(0)^2 - 3$
$= 0 - 3 = ③$

$x = 1$ $h(1) = 2(1)^2 - 3$
$= 2(1) - 3 = Ⓐ$

$x = 2$ $h(2) = 2(2)^2 - 3$
$= 2(4) - 3 = ⑤$

So, the range of *h*(*x*) is {15, 5, −1, −3, −1, 5}

(b) Complete the table

x	−4	−3	−2	−1	0	1	2
−*x*^{2}	−16	−9	−4	−1	0	−1	−4
−2*x*	8	6	4	2	0	−2	−4
+3	3	3	3	3	3	3	3
y	−5	0	3	4	3	0	−5

So, the points on the graph are
(−4, −5)(−3, 0)(−2, 3)(−1, 4)(0, 3)(1, 0)
(2, −5)

(i) *Solve for f(x) = 1.*

- Find the *x* values corresponding to *y* = 1.

  $\Rightarrow$ *x* = −2.7 and *x* = 0.7

65

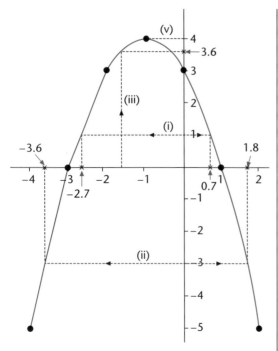

* Shown with line (i).

(ii) Solve for $-x^2 - 2x + 3 = -3$.

'Equation of the graph' = −3

$\Rightarrow \quad y = -3$

- Find the x values corresponding to $y = -3$.

$\Rightarrow \quad x = -3.6$ and $x = 1.8$

* Shown with line (ii).

(iii) Solve for $f(-1.5)$.

- Find the y value corresponding to $x = -1.5$.

$\Rightarrow y = 3.6$

* Shown with line (iii).

(iv) Solve for $f(0)$.

- Find the y value corresponding to $x = 0$.

$\Rightarrow y = 3$

(v) Find the maximum value of $f(x)$.

The maximum (largest) value of y is 4.

Chapter 7

Sample Paper One (with detailed solutions)

Question 1

(a) 20 people were asked to name their favourite holiday destination.

12 preferred Turkey
10 preferred Spain
11 preferred Portugal
5 liked Turkey and Portugal
6 liked Spain and Turkey
7 liked Spain and Portugal

If 4 liked all three destinations, complete a Venn diagram and hence calculate how many like none of the destinations.

(b) Copy the Venn diagram below and use a separate diagram to shade the following areas:

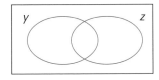

(i) $y \cap z$

(ii) $y \cup z$

(iii) y'

(iv) z/y

(v) $(y \cup z)'$

Question 2

(a) €2000 is lodged for three years at 15% compound interest. Calculate how much it amounts to at the end of that time.

(b) Evaluate the following, expressing your answer in the form $a \times 10^n$ where $1 \leqslant a < 10$ and $n \in N$.

(i) $\dfrac{(3.4 \times 10^3) \times (1.5 \times 10^4)}{1.7 \times 10^4}$

(ii) $6.8 \times 10^5 + 2.31 \times 10^3$

(c) €x is divided between Billy and Ruth in the ratio 2:3. If Billy receives €80, calculate:

(i) The amount Ruth received.

(ii) The value of x.

Question 3

(a) A bag costs €48.30, which includes 15% VAT. Evaluate:

(i) The cost of the bag before VAT was added on.

(ii) The cost of the bag if the percentage VAT was increased to 22%.

(b) Kieran earned a gross wage of €56,000 last year and had a standard rate cut-off of €30,000. His standard tax rate was 27% while his higher rate was 52%. If he had a tax credit of €7200 calculate:

(i) His gross tax.

(ii) His total tax paid.

(iii) Kieran's nett wage.

(c) Sheila buys a ring for €820 and later sells it for €1353. Calculate:

(i) The percentage profit made on the sale.

(ii) The selling price of the ring if it was sold for a 21% profit.

Question 4

(a) Mary is 5 years older than Tom. Twice Mary's age added to three times Tom's age is equal to 80 years.

(i) Let Tom's age = x and Mary's age = $x + 5$. Write an equation, to illustrate the information above.

(ii) Hence, find the age of Mary and Tom.

(b) Factorise the following:

(i) $4x^2 - 9x + 2$

(ii) $2m^2 + 4mp - 3mn - 6np$

(iii) $81x^2 - 16t^4$

Question 5

(a) Evaluate $3^3/_5 - 2^7/_{10} + 4^1/_4$

(b) (i) Simplify $\dfrac{2x - 1}{6} + \dfrac{4x - 3}{4}$

(ii) Hence, or otherwise, solve

$\dfrac{2x - 1}{6} + \dfrac{4x - 3}{4} = 3$

(c) Solve $3x - 1 > 2(3x + 4)$, $x \in R$ and illustrate your answer on the number line.

Question 6

(a) Given the function

$g: x \rightarrow 2x^2 - 4$

(i) Evaluate $g(-3)$

(ii) Evaluate $g(2t)$

(iii) Evaluate $g(4^1/_2)$

(iv) Solve for $g(-3n) = 14$

(b) Graph the function $f: x \rightarrow -2x^2 + 8x + 1$ in the domain $0 \leqslant x \leqslant 4$.

Let the graph represent the amount of people in a restaurant. The x-axis represents time from 11 a.m. ($x = 0$) and each gap along the axis being one hour. The y-axis represents the number of people with $x = 1$ being 10 people, $x = 2$ being 20 people etc.

Use the graph to find:

(i) How many people were in the restaurant at 11.30 a.m.?

(ii) At which times were there 80 people in the restaurant?

(iii) What was the greatest number of people at any one time in the restaurant?

(iv) At what time was the greatest number present?

Solutions to Sample Paper One

Solution to question 1

(a)	**Again, fill out the Venn diagram 'from the middle out'.**

'4 liked all three destinations'

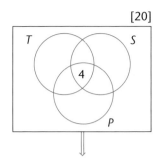

[20]

- 6 liked Turkey and Spain [6 – 4 = 2]
- 5 liked Turkey and Portugal [5 – 4 = 1]
- 7 liked Spain and Portugal [7 – 4 = 3]

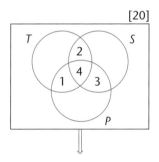

[20]

- *12 like Turkey* 12 – (2 + 4 + 1) = 5
- *10 like Spain* 10 – (2 + 4 + 3) = 1
- *11 like Portugal* 11 – (1 + 4 + 3) = 3

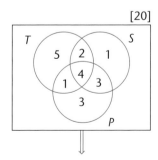

[20]

How many like none of the destinations?

$$5 + 2 + 1 + 1 + 4 + 3 + 3 = 19$$

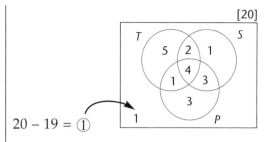

[20]

$20 – 19 = ①$

Therefore, one person likes none of the destinations.

(b)

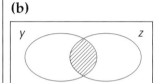

(i) $y \cap z$

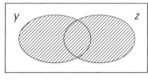

(ii) $y \cup z$

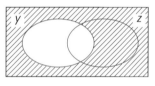

(iii) y'

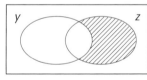

(iv) z/y

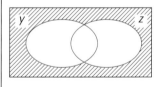

(v) $(y \cup z)'$

Solution to question 2

(a) €2000 is lodged for 3 years at 15% compound interest.

Year 1

Start €2000

69

Interest Earned

$\quad\quad$ 15% of €2000 = €300

End

$\quad\quad$ €2000 + €300 = €2300

Year 2

Start $\quad\quad\quad\quad$ €2300

Interest Earned

$\quad\quad$ 15% of €2300 = €345

End

$\quad\quad$ €2300 + €345 = €2645

Year 3

Start $\quad\quad\quad\quad$ €2645

Interest Earned

$\quad\quad$ 15% of €2645 = €396.75

End

$\quad\quad$ €2645 + €396.75 = €3041.75

So, €2000 amounted to €3041.75 after 3 years.

(b) Express the following in the form $a \times 10^n$ where $1 \leqslant a < 10$ and $n \in N$.

(i) $= \dfrac{(3.4 \times 10^3) \times (1.5 \times 10^4)}{1.7 \times 10^4}$

$\quad = \dfrac{3400 \times 15{,}000}{1700} = \dfrac{51{,}000{,}000}{1700}$

$\quad = 30{,}000$

$\quad = 3 \times 10^3$

(ii) $6.8 \times 10^5 + 2.31 \times 10^3$

$\quad\quad = 680{,}000 + 2310$

$\quad\quad = 682{,}310$

$\quad\quad = \underline{6.8231 \times 10^5}$

(c) €x is divided between Billy and Ruth in the ratio 2:3. Billy receives €80.

(i) *Calculate Ruth's share.*

Billy	:	Ruth
2	:	3
$\dfrac{2}{5}$	:	$\dfrac{3}{5}$

Billy receives $\dfrac{2}{5}$

$\Rightarrow \quad\quad\quad\quad €80 = \dfrac{2}{5}$

Calculate $\dfrac{1}{5}$

As $\quad\quad\quad\quad €80 = \dfrac{2}{5}$

$\quad\quad\quad\quad €80 \div 2 = \dfrac{1}{5}$

$\Rightarrow \quad\quad\quad\quad €40 = \dfrac{1}{5}$

So, Ruth received $\dfrac{3}{5}$

$\quad\quad\quad\quad = €40 \times 3$

$\quad\quad\quad\quad = \underline{€120}$

(ii) *Calculate x*

Total amount = €80 + €120

$\quad\quad\quad\quad = \underline{€200}$

Solution to question 3

(a) **A bag costs €48.30 which includes 15% VAT.**

(i) *Calculate the cost without VAT.*

$\quad\quad$ €48.30 includes 15% VAT

$\Rightarrow \quad\quad\quad\quad$ €48.30 = 115%

Find 1%

$$\frac{€48.30}{115} = 1\%$$

$$€0.42 = 1\%$$

Cost without VAT is always 100%

⇒ Cost without VAT

$$= €0.42 \times 100$$

$$= €42$$

(ii) *Find the cost with 22% VAT.*

Cost without VAT $= €42$

22% of €42 $= €9.24$

Cost including 22% VAT $= €51.24$

(b) (i) *Calculate his gross tax.*

$$\begin{array}{c} \text{Gross} \\ \text{Tax} \end{array} = \boxed{\begin{array}{c} 27\% \text{ of} \\ €30,000 \end{array}} + \boxed{\begin{array}{c} 52\% \text{ of} \\ €26,000 \end{array}}$$

$$[€56,000 - €30,000]$$

$$= €8100 + €13,520$$

So, Gross Tax $= €21,620$

(ii) Find the total tax paid.

Gross Tax – Tax credit = Tax paid

€21,260 – €7200 = Tax paid

So €14,060 = Tax paid

(iii) Find Kieran's Nett wage.

Nett wage = Gross wage – Tax paid

Nett wage = €56,000 – €14,060

$$= €41,940$$

(c) **Sheila buys a ring for €820 and sells it for €1353.**

(i) Cost price $= €820$

Selling price $= €1353$

⇒ Profit $= €1353 - €820$

$$= €533$$

% profit $= \dfrac{\text{Profit}}{\text{Cost price}} \times \dfrac{100}{1}$

⇒ % profit $= \dfrac{533}{820} \times \dfrac{100}{1}$

$$= 65\% \text{ profit}$$

(ii) Cost price $= €820$

21% of €820 $= + €172.20$

$$€992.20$$

So, if it was sold for a 21% profit the cost would be €992.20.

Solution to question 4

(a) **'Mary is 5 years older than Tom. Twice Mary's age added to three times Tom's age is equal to 80 years.'**

(i) $\underset{\underset{\text{Mary's age}}{\downarrow}}{2(x + 5)} + \underset{\underset{\text{Tom's age}}{\downarrow}}{3(x)} = 80$

⇒ $2x + 10 + 3x = 80$

$$2x + 3x = 80 - 10$$

$$5x = 70$$

$$x = \frac{70}{5}$$

⇒ $x = 14$

(ii) So, Tom is 14 years old and Mary is 19 years old.

(b) **(i) Factorise $4x^2 - 9x + 2$**

$$= (4x - 1)(x - 2)$$

(ii) Factorise $2m^2 + 4mp - 3mn - 6np$

⇒ $2m(m + 2p) - 3n(1m + 2p)$

$$= (2m - 3n)(m + 2p)$$

(iii) **Factorise $81x^2 - 16t^4$**

$$= (9x)^2 - (4t^2)^2$$

$$= \underline{(9x - 4t^2)(9x + 4t^2)}$$

Solution to question 5

(a) **Evaluate $3^3/_5 - 2^7/_{10} + 4^1/_4$**

$$3 - 2 + 4 = \underline{5}$$

$$\frac{3}{5} - \frac{7}{10} + \frac{1}{4}$$

$\boxed{LCM = 20} \Rightarrow \dfrac{12}{20} - \dfrac{14}{20} + \dfrac{5}{20} = \dfrac{3}{20}$

$\Rightarrow \qquad 3\dfrac{3}{5} - 2\dfrac{7}{10} + 4\dfrac{1}{4} = \boxed{5\dfrac{3}{20}}$

(b) **(i) Simplify $\dfrac{2x - 1}{6} + \dfrac{4x - 3}{4}$**

$\boxed{LCM = 12}$

$\Rightarrow \qquad \dfrac{12(2x - 1)}{6} + \dfrac{12(4x - 3)}{4}$

$= \dfrac{2(2x - 1) + 3(4x - 3)}{12}$

$= \dfrac{4x - 2 + 12x - 9}{12} = \boxed{\dfrac{16x - 11}{12}}$

(ii) **Hence, or otherwise, solve**

$$\dfrac{2x - 1}{6} + \dfrac{4x - 3}{4} = 3$$

$\Rightarrow \qquad \dfrac{16x - 11}{12} = 3$

$$\dfrac{16x - 11}{12} = \dfrac{3}{1}$$

$\boxed{LCM = 12} \qquad \dfrac{12(16x - 11)}{12} = \dfrac{12(3)}{1}$

$$1(16x - 11) = 12(3)$$

$$16x - 11 = 36$$

$$16x = 36 + 11$$

$$16x = 47$$

$$x = \dfrac{47}{16} \Rightarrow \boxed{x = 2^{15}/_{16}}$$

(c) **Solve $3x - 1 > 2(3x + 4)$, $x \in R$ and illustrate your answer.**

$\Rightarrow \qquad\qquad 3x - 1 > 6x + 8$

$$3x - 6x > 8 + 1$$

$$-3x > 9$$

x is negative $\Rightarrow 3x < -9$

$$\boxed{x < -3}, x \in R$$

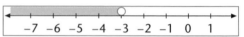

Solution to question 6

(a) $g: x \rightarrow 2x^2 - 4$

(i) *Find $g(-3)$*

$$g(-3) = 2(-3)^2 - 4$$

$$= 18 - 4$$

$$= \underline{14}$$

(ii) *Find $g(2t)$*

$$g(2t) = 2(2t)^2 - 4$$

$\boxed{\text{Again, please work out } (2t)^2 \text{ first.}}$

$$= 2(4t^2) - 4$$

$$= 8t^2 - 4$$

(iii) *Find $g(4^1/_2)$*

$$g(4.5) = 2(4.5)^2 - 4$$

$$= 2(20.25) - 4$$

$$= 40.50 - 4$$

$$= 36.50$$

(iv) *Solve for $g(-3n) = 14$*

Find $g(-3n)$

$$g(-3n) = 2(-3n)^2 - 4$$

$$= 2(9n^2) - 4$$

$$= 18n^2 - 4$$

Solve for n

$$18n^2 - 4 = 14$$
$$18n^2 = 14 + 4$$
$$18n^2 = 18$$
$$n^2 = {}^{18}/_{18}$$
$$n^2 = 1$$
$$n = \sqrt{1}$$

So $\qquad n = 1$ and $n = -1$

(b) Complete the table

x	0	1	2	3	4
$-2x^2$	0	-2	-8	-18	-32
$+8x$	0	8	16	24	32
$+1$	1	1	1	1	1
y	1	7	9	7	1

The points of the graph are $(0, 1)$ $(1, 7)$
$(2, 9)$ $(3, 7)$ $(4, 1)$

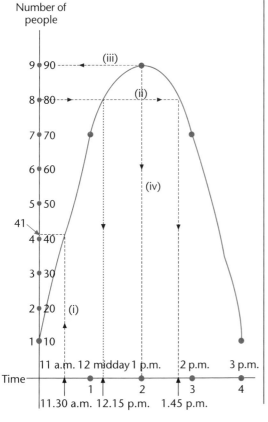

(i) How many people were in the restaurant at 11.30 a.m.?

41 people

*Shown by line (i)

(ii) At which times were there 80 people in the restaurant?

At 12.15 p.m. and 1.45 p.m.

* Shown by line (ii)

(iii) What was the greatest number of people at any one time in the restaurant?

90 people

*Shown by line (iii)

(iv) At what time was the greatest number present?

At 1 pm

* Shown by line (iv)

73

Chapter 8
Area and Volume

All the formulas relating to Area and Volume you will need can be found on page 9 of the log tables. We will now look at these formulas and some important questions based on each formula.

Section A
Area and Perimeter

Important

'Perimeter' and 'Length' are always measured in mm, cm or m. 'Area' is always measured in mm², cm² or m².

① *The square and rectangle*

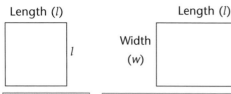

Area = $l \times l$	Area = $l \times w$
Perimeter = $4l$	Perimeter = $2l + 2w$
	= $2(l + w)$

Example 1

The width of a rectangle is 8 cm and it has a perimeter of 40 cm. Calculate the length of the rectangle.

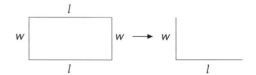

perimeter = 40 cm $\Rightarrow$ $l + w$ = 20 cm

length + width = 20 cm
length + 8 cm = 20 cm
<u>So, length = 12 cm</u>

Example 2

A kitchen floor is 8 m in length and 5 m wide. How many square tiles of length 25 cm would it take to cover the floor?

• Find the area of the floor.

• Find the area of a tile.

• Number of tiles $= \dfrac{\text{Area of the floor}}{\text{Area of a tile}}$

Area of the floor = $l \times w$
$$= 8 \text{ m} \times 5 \text{ m}$$
$$= 800 \text{ cm} \times 500 \text{ cm}$$
$$= 400{,}000 \text{ cm}^2$$

Area of a tile = $l \times l$
$$= 25 \times 25$$
$$= 625 \text{ cm}^2$$

Number of tiles $= \dfrac{400{,}000}{625} = \underline{640}$

So, it would take 640 tiles to cover the floor.

Example 3

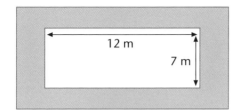

John's back garden is 12 m long and 7 m wide. It is sorrounded by paving 50 cm wide. Calculate:

(i) The total area of the paving.

(ii) If paving stones cost €4 per m², find the cost of the paving stones.

(i)

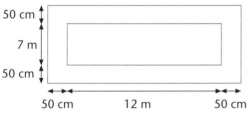

Area of large rectangle

$$= \text{length} \times \text{width}$$

$$= 13 \text{ m} \times 8 \text{ m}$$

$$= 104 \ m^2$$

Area of inner rectangle = 12×7 m

$$= 84 \ m^2$$

⇒ Area of footpath = 104 m² – 84 m²

$$= \underline{20 \ m^2}$$

(ii) Cost of the footpath = 20×4

$$= \underline{€80}$$

② *Triangle and parallelogram*

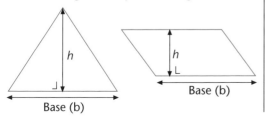

Triangle

Area = $\frac{1}{2}$ (base) × (perpendicular height) = $\frac{1}{2}$ bh

Parallelogram

Area = base × perpendicular height = $b \times h$

Example 1

The area of the triangle here is 35 cm². Calculate h.

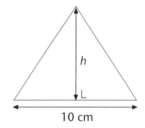

Area = $\frac{1}{2}$ (base) × (perpendicular height)

⇒ $\quad\quad 35 = \frac{1}{2}$ (10) × h

⇒ $\quad\quad 35 = 5h$

$\quad\quad \frac{35}{5} = h$ <u>So, $h = 7$ cm</u>

Example 2

This parallelogram has an area of 36 cm². Find h.

Area = Base × Perpendicular height

⇒ $\quad\quad 36 = 8 \times h$

$\quad\quad \frac{36}{8} = h$ <u>So, $h = 4.5$ cm</u>

③ *Circle and sector of a circle*

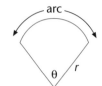

Area = πr^2 Circumference = $2\pi r$	Area $= \dfrac{\theta}{360} \times \pi r^2$ Length of arc $= \dfrac{\theta}{360} \times 2\pi r$

Circumference is 'length' in the log tables.

Example 1

Calculate

(i) The area of the sector *abc*.

(ii) The length of the arc *ac*.

$$\left(\text{let } \pi = \frac{22}{7}\right)$$

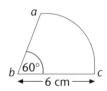

(i) Area $= \dfrac{\theta}{360} \times \pi r^2$

$\qquad = \dfrac{60}{360} \times \dfrac{22}{7} \times 6 \times 6$

$\qquad = \boxed{60 \; a^b/_c \; 360 \times 22 \; a^b/_c \; 7 \times 6 \times 6}$

$\qquad = 18.86$

So, $\qquad$ area = 18.86 cm^2

(ii) Length of arc $= \dfrac{\theta}{360} \times 2\pi r$

$\qquad = \dfrac{60}{360} \times 2 \times \dfrac{22}{7} \times 6$

$\qquad = 6.3$

So, length of arc *ac* = 6.3 cm

Example 2

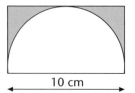

10 cm

A semicircle is cut out of a rectangulr piece of card as shown. Calculate:

(i) The area of the semicircle. (let π = 3.14)

(ii) The area of card remaining.

(iii) The percentage of card remaining.

(i)

5 cm

Area of semicircle = $\dfrac{1}{2}$ (area of full circle)

$\Rightarrow \qquad$ Area $= \dfrac{1}{2} \; (\pi r^2)$

$\qquad\qquad = \dfrac{1}{2} \times 3.14 \times 5 \times 5$

$\qquad\qquad = 39.25$

$\Rightarrow \qquad$ Area = 39.25 cm^2

(ii)

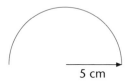

5 cm

5 cm — 5 cm

$\qquad$ Area = $l \times w$

$\qquad\qquad = 10 \times 5$

$\qquad\qquad = 50$ cm^2

$\Rightarrow \qquad$ Area of card remaining

$\qquad\qquad = 50$ cm^2 – 39.25 cm^2 = 10.75 cm^2

(iii)

$$\text{\% of card remaining} = \frac{\text{Amount of card remaining}}{\text{Total amount of card at the start}} \times \frac{100}{1}$$

$$= \frac{10.75}{50} \times \frac{100}{1}$$

$$= 21.5$$

$\Rightarrow$ Percentage of card remaining

$$= \underline{21.5\%}$$

Example 3

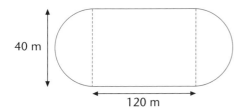

40 m

120 m

A running track with given dimensions is shown above. Calculate:

(i) The area of the track. (let $\pi = {}^{22}/_7$)

(ii) The total length around the track.

(iii) How many laps a runner would complete in a 3000 m race.

(i) | Area of track = area of semicircles + area of middle rectangle |

① Area of 2 semicircles = Area of 1 circle (radius 20 m)

Area of circle = πr^2

$$= \frac{22}{7} \times 20 \times 20$$

$$= 1257.14 \ m^2$$

② Area of rectangle = $l \times w$

$$= 120 \text{ m} \times 40 \text{ m}$$

$$= 4800 \ m^2$$

Area of runnning track = 1257.14 m² + 4800 m²

$$= \underline{6057.14 \ m^2}$$

(ii)

| Length of track = 'Length' of the 2 semicircles + 120 m + 120 m |

Length of 2 semicircles = length (circumference) of 1 circle (radius 20 m)

Circumference of circle = $2\pi r$

$$= 2 \times \frac{22}{7} \times 20$$

$$= 125.7 \text{ m}$$

$\Rightarrow$ Length of running track

$$= 125.7 \text{ m} + 120 \text{ m} + 120 \text{ m}$$

$$= \underline{365.7 \text{ m}}$$

(iii) | $\text{Number of laps in race} = \frac{\text{Length of race}}{\text{Length of track}}$ |

$\Rightarrow$ Number of laps in 3000 m race $= \frac{3000}{365.7}$

$$= \underline{8.2}$$

$\Rightarrow$ 8.2 laps are completed in a 3000 m race.

③ *Given the area or circumference of a circle and asked to find the radius.*

Example 1

The area of a circle is 78.57 cm². Find the radius of the circle. (let $\pi = {}^{22}/_7$)

Important

When you are told the area or the circumference of a circle and asked to find the radius *please* follow these steps.

① **Let the area formula = 78.57**

$\Rightarrow \qquad \pi r^2 = 78.57$

② **Evaluate as much as you can.**

$$\pi r^2 = 78.57$$

$\Rightarrow \qquad \dfrac{22}{7} \times r^2 = 78.57$

③ • **Leave r^2 on the left.**

• **Bring $\dfrac{22}{7}$ across and divide it into 78.57**

$$r^2 = 78.57 \div \left(\dfrac{22}{7} \right)$$

$$\boxed{= 78.57 \div (22\ \boxed{a^b/_c}\ 7)}$$

$$= 25$$

So, $\qquad r^2 = 25$

$$r = \sqrt{25}$$

$$= 5$$

So, the radius is 5 cm.

Example 2

The circumference of a circle is 44 cm. Calculate its radius.

① **Let the circumference formula = 44.**

$\Rightarrow \qquad 2\pi r = 44$

② Evaluate as much as you can.

$$2 \times \dfrac{22}{7} \times r = 44$$

• Leave r on the left.

• Bring the other 2 numbers across and divide them into 44.

$$r = 44 \div 2 \div \left(\dfrac{22}{7} \right)$$

$$\boxed{44 \div 2 \div (22\ \boxed{a^b/_c}\ 7)}$$

$$= 7$$

So, the radius is 7 cm.

Section B
Volume and Surface Area

Important

'Volume' is always measured in mm³, cm³ or m³.

① **Rectangular blocks and cubes**

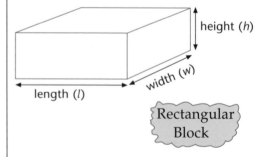

length (*l*)   width (w)   height (*h*)

Rectangular Block

Volume = $l \times w \times h$

Surface Area = $2lh + 2lw + 2hw$

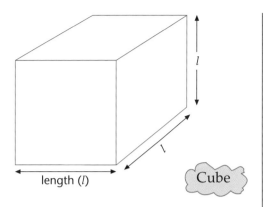

length (*l*)

Cube

Volume = $l \times l \times l$

Surface area = $6l^2$

Example 1

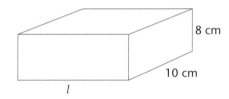

8 cm

10 cm

l

The volume of this rectangular block is 1200 cm^3. Calculate:

(i) The length of the block.

(ii) The surface area of the block.

(i) Volume = 1200 cm^3

So, let volume formula = 1200

$\Rightarrow \qquad l \times w \times h = 1200$

$l \times 10 \times 8 = 1200$

So, $\qquad l = 1200 \div 10 \div 8$

$l = 15$

So, <u>length = 15 cm</u>

(ii) Surface area = $2lh + 2lw + 2hw$

$= 2(15)(8) + 2(15)(10) + 2(8)(10)$

$= 240 + 300 + 160$

$= 700$

So, <u>surface area = 700 cm^2</u>

Example 2

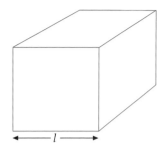

l

The cube here has a surface area of 294 cm^2. Calculate:

(i) The length of one side of the cube.

(ii) The volume of the cube.

(i) Surface area = 294 cm^2

$\Rightarrow \qquad\qquad 6l^2 = 294$

$\Rightarrow \qquad\qquad 6 \times l^2 = 294$

$l^2 = 294 \div 6$

$l^2 = 49$

So, $\qquad\qquad l = \sqrt{49}$

$l = 7$

So, length of each side is 7 cm.

(ii) Volume = l^3

$= 7^3$

$= 343$

So, the Volume of the cube is 343 cm^3.

② The cylinder and the sphere

Cylinder

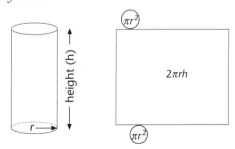

height (h)

r

πr^2

$2\pi rh$

πr^2

Volume = $\pi r^2 h$

Curved surface area = $2\pi rh$

Total surface area = $2\pi rh + 2\pi r^2$

Sphere

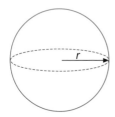

Volume = $\dfrac{3}{4}\pi r^3$

Curved surface area = $4\pi r^2$

Question *Type 1*
'In terms of π'

Note

When we are asked to calculate the volume or area of an object 'in terms of π':

① Fill out the formula for all values except π. Do not substitute 3.14 or $\dfrac{22}{7}$ for π.

② Your final answer will therefore include π.

Example

A cylinder has a radius of 8 cm and a height of 12 cm. Calculate:

(i) The volume of the cylinder in terms of π.

(ii) The total surface area in terms of π.

(i) Volume = $\pi r^2 h$

| Let $r = 8$, $h = 12$ and $\pi = \pi$. |

$= \pi \times 8 \times 8 \times 12$

$= \underline{768\pi}$

(ii) Total surface area $2\pi rh + 2\pi r^2$

$= (2 \times \pi \times 8 \times 12) + (2 \times \pi \times 8 \times 8)$

$= 192\pi + 128\pi$

$= \underline{320\pi}$

Question *Type 2*
'Items being packed'

In the following three examples, the diagram is very important. Read the notes which accompany the questions carefully and this type of question will be very manageable.

Example 1

Three spheres of radius 6 cm are packed into a cylinder. Calculate:

(i) The volume of the cylinder.

(ii) The volume of empty space in the cylinder. (let $\pi = 3.14$)

Dimensions of the cylinder

*Please remember that the radius of each sphere is 6 cm, so diameter is 12 cm.

*Radius of cylinder = radius of sphere

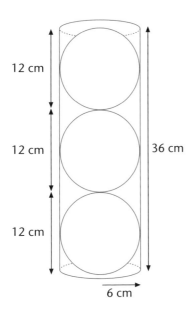

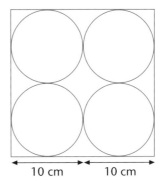

(i) Volume of cylinder = $\pi r^2 h$

$$= 3.14 \times 6 \times 6 \times 36$$

$$= \underline{4069.44 \text{ cm}^3}$$

(ii) Volume of sphere = $^4/_3 \, \pi r^3$

$$= (^4/_3) \times 3.14 \times 6 \times 6 \times 6$$

$$= 904.32 \text{ cm}^3$$

$\Rightarrow$ Volume of 3 spheres = 904.32×3

$$= \underline{2712.96 \text{ cm}^3}$$

Volume of empty space =

Volume of cylinder – Volume of spheres

Vol. of empty space

$$= 4069.44 - 2712.96$$

$$= \underline{1356.48 \text{ cm}^3}$$

Example 2

Four cylinders of radius 5 cm and height 14 cm are packed into a rectangular box. Calculate the volume of the box.

Cylinders packed into a rectangular box … think of a packet of cigarettes.

*Height of box = height of cylinders

*Width and length of box shown here.

So, Height = 14 cm (same as cylinders)

Width = 20 cm, Length = 20 cm

Volume = $l \times w \times h$

$$= 20 \times 20 \times 14$$

$$= \underline{5600 \text{ cm}^3}$$

Note

Arranging the cylinders like this would yield the same answer.

Example 3

Three spheres of radius 4 cm are packed into a rectangular box. Calculate the volume of the box.

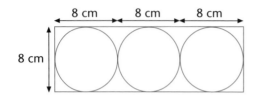

Height of this box = diameter of the spheres (8 cm)

*The width and length of the box are shown above.

So, Height = 8 cm, Width = 8 cm

Length = 24 cm

Volume = $l \times w \times h$

$= 24 \times 8 \times 8$

$= 1536 \ cm^3$

Question *Type 3*
Questions involving liquid

Example 1

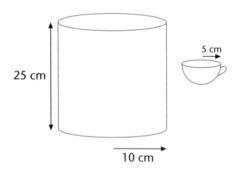

A cup in the shape of a hemisphere (radius 5 cm) is filled and emptied into the cylindrical tank. Find how many times the cup must be filled

and emptied into the tank in order to fill the tank. $\left(\text{let } \pi = \frac{22}{7} \right)$

① **Volume of cylinder**

Volume = $\pi r^2 h$

$= \frac{22}{7} \times 10 \times 10 \times 25$

$= 7857.14 \ cm^3$

② **Volume of hemisphere**

Note

The volume of a hemisphere is *not* in the log tables.

Vol. of sphere	Vol. of hemisphere
$\frac{4}{3} \pi r^3$	$\frac{2}{3} \pi r^3$

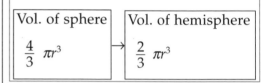

$\Rightarrow \qquad \frac{2}{3} \pi r^3$

$= \frac{2}{3} \times \frac{22}{7} \times 5 \times 5 \times 5$

$= 261.9 \ cm^3$

Number of times it must be emptied in	=	Volume of cylinder
		Volume of hemisphere

$= \frac{7857.14}{261.9}$

$= 30$

So, the cup wil have to be filled and emptied 30 times to fill the tank.

Example 2

Question 1

A cylinder of radius 15 cm contains 7065 cm³ of water. Calculate the height of water in the cylinder. (let π = 3.14)

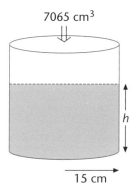

7065 cm³

15 cm

Volume of liquid = Formula for the container

$$7065 = \pi r^2 h$$
$$7065 = 3.14 \times 15 \times 15 \times h$$
$$7065 \div 3.14 \div 15 \div 15 = h$$
$$10 = h$$

So, the height of water is 10 cm.

Question 2

A rectangular tank of length 15 cm and width 10 cm contains 2.1 litres of water. Calculate the height of water in the tank.

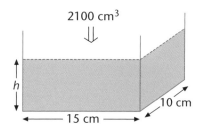

2100 cm³

h

15 cm

10 cm

Important

$$1 \text{ litre} = 1000 \text{ cm}^3$$
$$\Rightarrow 2.1 \text{ litres} = 2100 \text{ cm}^3$$

Volume of liquid = Formula for the container

$$2100 = l \times w \times h$$
$$2100 = 15 \times 10 \times h$$
$$2100 \div 15 \div 10 = h$$
$$14 = h$$

So, the height of water is 14 cm.

Example 3

A very popular question is one in which we are given the area or volume of an item and we are asked to find the radius of the height.

Please follow the steps outlined below carefully and you will see that these questions are quite straightforward.

Question 1

The volume of a cylinder is 628 cm³. Its height is 8 cm, find its radius. (let π = 3.14)

① Let the volume formula = 628

Volume of cylinder = $\pi r^2 h$

$\Rightarrow$ $\pi r^2 h = 628$

> ② **Fill out the formula as much as you can.**

$$3.14 \times r^2 \times 8 = 628$$

> ③ **Leave r^2 on the left. Bring the other across to the right and divide them into 628.**

$$r^2 = 628 \div 3.14 \div 8$$
$$r^2 = 25$$
$$r = \sqrt{25}$$
$$\underline{r = 5 \text{ cm}}$$

Question 2

The volume of a sphere is 1437.33 cm³. Calculate its radius.

$$\left(\text{let } \pi = \frac{22}{7} \right)$$

> ① Let the volume formula = 1437.33

Volume of sphere $= \frac{4}{3} \pi r^3$

$\Rightarrow$ $\frac{4}{3} \pi r^3 = 1437.33$

> ② Fill out the formula as much as you can.

$$\frac{4}{3} \times \frac{22}{7} \times r^3 = 1437.33$$

> ③ Divide the right-hand side by $^4/_3$ and by $^{22}/_7$.
>
> *When you divide by a fraction, it is advisable to leave it in brackets.

$$r^3 = 1437.33 \div \left(\frac{4}{3}\right) \div \left(\frac{22}{7}\right)$$

$$r^3 = 343$$

$$r = \sqrt[3]{343}$$

> | 2nd F | √ | | 343 |

$$= 7$$

So, the radius is 7 cm.

Question 3

The curved surface area of a cylinder is 96π cm³. Its radius is 6 cm, calculate its height.

> ① Let the curved surface area formula = 96π

Curved surface area of a cylinder = $2\pi r h$

$\Rightarrow$ $2\pi r h = 96\pi$

> ** Cancel the π on each side **

$$2\pi\!\!\!/ r h = 96\pi\!\!\!/$$

So, $2rh = 96$

> ② Fill out the equation as much as you can.

$$2 \times 6 \times h = 96$$

> ③ Divide the right-hand side by 2 and by 6.

$$h = 96 \div 2 \div 6$$
$$h = 8$$

So, the height is 8 cm.

Chapter 8
Sample questions for you to try

Question 1

(a) Seán cuts a piece of wire 56.55 cm in length. He makes the rim of a wheel from the wire. (let $\pi = \frac{22}{7}$) Calculate:

(i) The radius of the wheel.

(ii) How many times must the wheel rotate along the road in order to travel a distance of 113.1 m.

(b)

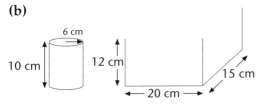

A cylindrical jar has radius 6 cm and height 10 cm. It is used to fill the given rectangular tank with water. Calculate:

(i) The volume of the jar. (let $\pi = 3.14$)

(ii) The volume of the tank.

(iii) The number of times the jar will have to be filled up and emptied into the tank in order to fill it.

Question 2

(a) A large rectangular tank of length 1.1 m, height 60 cm and width 30 cm is used to hold cubes with sides of 10 cm. How many cubes could fit in the tank?

(b)

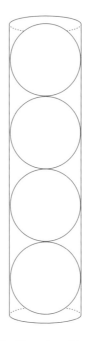

Four tennis balls of radius 3 cm are kept in a cylindrical tube. Calculate:

(i) The volume of the cylinder. $\left(\text{let } \pi = \frac{22}{7}\right)$

(ii) The volume of the four tennis balls.

(iii) The percentage of empty space in the tube.

Question 3

(a)

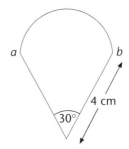

Calculate:

(i) The area of the sector in terms of π.

(ii) the length of arc ab in terms of π.

(b) A cylindrical tank has a radius of 10 cm. 2512 cm³ of water is emptied into the tank. Calculate (to the nearest cm) the height of water in the tank. (let $\pi = 3.14$)

(c) **(i)** A cylinder has a volume of 628.32 cm³. If its height is 8 cm, calculate its radius correct to the nearest whole number. $\left(\text{let } \pi = \dfrac{22}{7}\right)$

(ii) Hence find the total surface area of the cylinder.

Solution to question 1

(a)

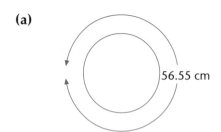

$\Rightarrow$ **Circumference of wheel = 56.55 cm**

(i) Circumference = 56.55 cm

$\Rightarrow$ $\qquad 2\pi r = 56.55$

$2 \times \dfrac{22}{7} \times r = 56.55$

$r = 56.55 \div 2 \div \left(\dfrac{22}{7}\right)$

$\Rightarrow \qquad r = 9$

<u>So, radius is 9 cm.</u>

(ii)

> As the circumference is 56.55 cm, the wheel will travel 56.55 cm if it rotates once on the road.

$\Rightarrow$ Number of rotations to travel 113.1 m $= \dfrac{113.1 \text{ m}}{56.55 \text{ cm}}$

$= \dfrac{11{,}310 \text{ cm}}{56.55 \text{ cm}}$

$= 200$

Therefore the wheel would rotate 200 times.

(b) **(i)**

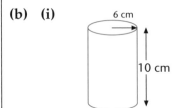

Volume of cylinder
$= \pi r^2 h$
$= 3.14 \times 6 \times 6 \times 10$
$= \underline{113.04 \text{ cm}^3}$

(ii) Volume of the tank $= l \times w \times h$
$= 20 \times 15 \times 12$
$= \underline{3600 \text{ cm}^3}$

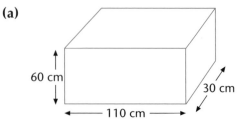

(iii) $\dfrac{\text{Volume of tank}}{\text{Volume of jar}} = \dfrac{3600}{113.04}$

$= 31.85$

So, it would have to be emptied into the tank 32 times in order to fill it.

Solution to question 2

(a)

Volume of rectangular block = $l \times w \times h$

$$= 110 \text{ cm} \times 30 \text{ cm} \times 60 \text{ cm}$$

$$= 198{,}000 \text{ cm}^3$$

10 cm

Volume of cube = l^3

$$= 10^3$$

$$= 1000 \text{ cm}^3$$

Number of cubes that would fit $= \dfrac{\textbf{Volume of the rec. block}}{\textbf{Volume of each cube}}$

$$= \frac{198{,}000}{1000}$$

$$= 198$$

So, 198 cubes would fit in the rectangular block.

(b)

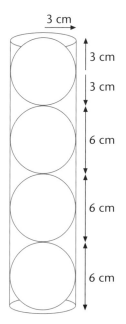

3 cm

3 cm

3 cm

6 cm

6 cm

6 cm

(i) Volume of the cylinder

$$= \pi r^2 h$$

$$= \frac{22}{7} \times 3 \times 3 \times 24$$

$$= 678.58 \text{ cm}^3$$

(ii) Volume of sphere $= \dfrac{4}{3}\,\pi r^3$

$$= \frac{4}{3} \times \frac{22}{7} \times 3 \times 3 \times 3$$

$$= 113.1 \text{ cm}^3$$

$\Rightarrow$ Volume of the 4 spheres

$$= 113.1 \times 4$$

$$= \underline{452.4 \text{ cm}^3}$$

(iii) Amount of empty space

= volume of cylinder

– volume of spheres

$$= 678.58 \text{ cm}^3 - 452.4 \text{ cm}^3$$

$$= 226.18 \text{ cm}^3$$

% of empty space	$= \dfrac{\textbf{Vol. of empty space}}{\textbf{Vol. of cylinder}} \times \dfrac{\textbf{100}}{\textbf{1}}$

$$\frac{\% \text{ of empty}}{\text{space}} = \frac{226.18}{678.58} \times \frac{100}{1}$$

$$= \underline{33^1/_3\%}$$

Solution to question 3

(a)

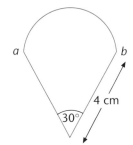

a b

4 cm

30°

(i) area of the sector $= \dfrac{\theta}{360} \times \pi r^2$

> Again because we are asked to find the area 'in terms of π' do not substitute a number for π in the formula.

$\Rightarrow \qquad$ Area $= \dfrac{30}{360} \times \pi \times 4 \times 4$

$\qquad\qquad\quad = \underline{1.33\ \pi}$

(ii) Length of arc ab

$\qquad\qquad = \dfrac{\theta}{360} \times 2\pi r$

$\qquad\qquad = \dfrac{30}{360} \times 2 \times \pi \times 4$

$\qquad\qquad = \underline{0.67\ \pi}$

(b)

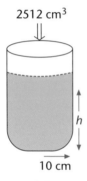

2512 cm³

h

10 cm

> let Volume of liquid = formula for container

$\qquad 2512 = \pi r^2 h$

$\qquad 2512 = 3.14 \times 10 \times 10 \times h$

$\Rightarrow \quad 2512 \div 3.14 \div 10 \div 10 = h$

$\Rightarrow \qquad\qquad\qquad 8 = h$

So, the water was 8 cm high.

(c)

(i) Volume of cylinder = 628.32

$\Rightarrow \qquad\qquad \pi r^2 h = 628.32$

$\dfrac{22}{7} \times r^2 \times 8 = 628.32$

$r^2 = 628.32 \div \left(\dfrac{22}{7}\right) \div 8$

$r^2 = 25$

$r = \sqrt{25}$

$\underline{r = 5\ \text{cm}}$

(ii) Total surface area

$= 2\pi r h + 2\pi r^2$

$= \left(2 \times \dfrac{22}{7} \times 5 \times 8\right) + \left(2 \times \dfrac{22}{7} \times 5 \times 5\right)$

$= 251.43 + 157.14$

$= 408.57$

So, total surface area is

$\qquad\qquad 408.57\ \text{cm}^2.$

Chapter 9
Congruent Triangles and Transformations

Section A

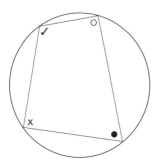

When a circle contains a four-sided figure as shown, the opposite angles add up to 180°.

$$(\checkmark) + (\bullet) = 180°$$
$$(x) + (\circ) = 180°$$

Example

Evaluate p and r.

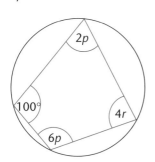

The opposite angles add up to 180°.

$\Rightarrow \qquad 100° + 4r = 180°$

$4r = 180° - 100°$

$4r = 80°$

$\Rightarrow \qquad r = 20°$

$\Rightarrow \qquad 2p + 6p = 180°$

$\qquad 8p = 180°$

$\qquad p = \dfrac{180°}{8}$

$\Rightarrow \qquad p = 22\dfrac{1}{2}°$

Section B
Translations

Under a translation, the object moves along a given straight line.

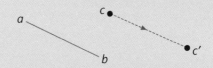

Here the image of pt. c under the translation $\overrightarrow{ab}$ is c'.

Note

c' is found by 'translating' point c:

① In the same direction.

② The same distance

$\qquad$ as $\overrightarrow{ab}$.

Example 1

Find the image of M under the translation $\overrightarrow{cd}$.

Solution

- Mark the five main points on M.
- Find the image of each pt. under $\overrightarrow{cd}$.

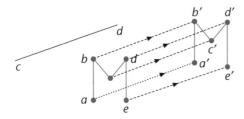

Example 2

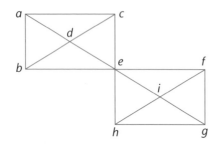

Find the image of:

① [ab] under $\overrightarrow{hg}$ [Point h is translated onto point g]

$\left.\begin{array}{l} a \to c \\ b \to e \end{array}\right\}$ Look at $\overrightarrow{hg}$. Bring both pt. a and pt. b in the same direction, the same distance.

⇒ **Image of [ab] under $\overrightarrow{hg}$ is [ce].**

② **△acd under $\overrightarrow{bh}$**

$a \to e$ ⇒ image of △acd

$c \to f$ **under $\overrightarrow{bh}$ is △efi**

$d \to i$

③ **△abd under $\overrightarrow{cf}$**

$a \to e$ ⇒ image of △abd

$b \to h$ **under $\overrightarrow{cf}$ is △ehi**

$d \to i$

Example 3

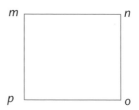

Construct the image of the square under the translation $\overrightarrow{mn}$.

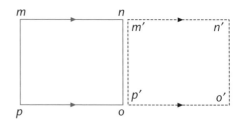

Under the translation $\overrightarrow{mn}$ each of the four points m, n, p, o are translated:

① In the same direction.

② The same distance as $\overrightarrow{mn}$.

Therefore $m \to m'$, $n \to n'$, $p \to p'$ and $o \to o'$ as in diagram.

Section C
Axial Symmetry

Under axial symmetry, the object is reflected across a line.

Here the image of pt. c under S_A, an axial symmetry in the line A, is c', To find c':

① From pt. c draw a perpendicular line onto A.

② Carry on the same distance the other side.

Example 1

Find the image of T under S_B, an axial symmetry in line B.

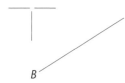

Solution

Again, we mark the four main points onto T and find the image of each.

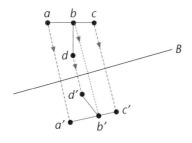

Example 2

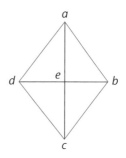

Find the image of:

(i) *[ad] under $S_{[ac]}$, an axial symmetry in [ac]*

$a \rightarrow a \quad \Rightarrow$ Image of $[ad]$ under

$d \rightarrow b \qquad S_{[ac]}$ is [ab]

> *The image of pt. a under $S_{[ac]}$ is a. This is because pt. a is <u>on</u> the line $[ac]$.

(ii) *△ebc under $S_{[db]}$ an axial symmetry in [db]*

$e \rightarrow e$

$b \rightarrow b \qquad \Rightarrow$ The image of $\triangle ebc$

$c \rightarrow a \qquad$ under $S_{[db]}$ is $\triangle$eba

Example 3

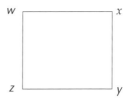

Construct the image of the square under $S_{[zy]}$, an axial symmetry in the line $[zy]$.

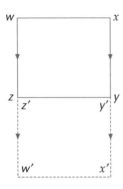

Section D
Central Symmetry

Under central symmetry, the object is reflected through a fixed point.

Here, the image of pt. a under S_b, a central symmetry in pt. b is a'. To find a':

① Draw a line from a to b.
② Carry on again the same distance the other side.

Example 1

Find the image of F under S_w, a central symmetry in pt. w.

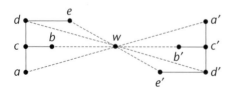

Solution

Again, mark in the five main points onto F and find the image of each.

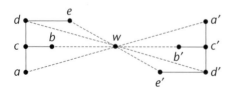

Example 2

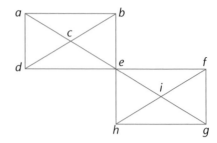

Find the image of:

(i) [ad] under S_c, a central symmetry in pt. c.

$a \rightarrow e$ $\Rightarrow$ Image of [ad] under
$d \rightarrow b$ S_c is [eb]

(ii) $\triangle dbe$ under S_e, a central symmetry in pt. e.

$d \rightarrow f$

$b \rightarrow h$ | *The image of pt. e under S_e is itself.

$e \rightarrow e$

$\Rightarrow$ Image of $\triangle dbe$ under S_e is $\underline{\triangle fhe}$

Example 3

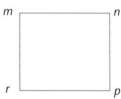

Construct the image of the square under Sp, a central symmetry in the point p.

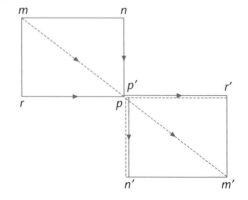

From each of the four points, we draw a construction line through point *p*.

What does it mean if two triangles are congruent?

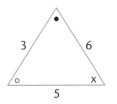 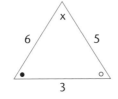

If two triangles are congruent…

The measure of all sides and angles in the first triangle are equal to the measure of all *corresponding* sides and angles in the second triangle. Two sides are corresponding when they are opposite equal angles.

How can we prove two triangles are congruent?

① *SAS*

When *2 sides and the angle in between them* in one triangle are equal to 2 sides and the angle in between them in the other triangle.

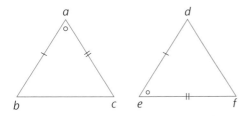

△*abc* and △*def* are congruent because of *SAS*.

② *AAS*

When *2 angles and a side* in one triangle are equal to 2 angles and the *corresponding* side in the other triangle.

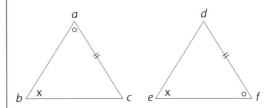

Important

*Always mark in equal angles using x, ○ or •

△*abe* and △*def* are congruent because of *AAS*.

③ *SSS*

When the *3 sides* in one triangle are equal to the 3 sides in the other triangle.

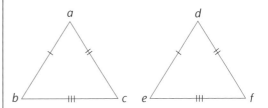

△*abc* and △*def* are congruent because of *SSS*.

④ **RHS**

When the ***Right-angle, Hypothenuse and Second side*** in the two triangles are equal.

△*abc* and △*def* are congruent because of *RHS*.

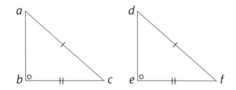

We prove that two triangles are congruent therefore if we show *any* <u>one</u> of the following:

① SAS

② AAS

③ SSS

④ RHS

Example

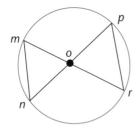

Investigate whether △*mon* and △*por* are congruent.

Please follow the three steps outlined here for all congruent triangle questions.

① **Investigate if any side in △*mon* is equal to a side in △*por*. (You *must* be able to give a reason.)**

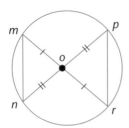

(i) $|mo| = |or|$ ... both radii

(ii) $|no| = |op|$ ... both radii

② **Investigate if any angle in △*mon* is equal to an angle in △*por*. (Again, you must be able to say why.)**

$|\angle mon| = |\angle por|$ ... vertically opposite.

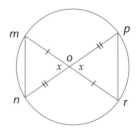

③ **Investigate if △*mon* is congruent to △*pon*.**

From the above diagram, we see that the triangles *are* congruent because of <u>SAS</u>.

Question 1

(a)

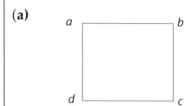

Construct the image of the square above under S_c, a central symmetry in point *c*.

(b)

Find the image of:

(i) $\triangle kgh$ under S_k, a central symmetry in point k.

(ii) $[ej]$ under $S_{[fi]}$, an axial symmetry in the line $[fi]$.

(iii) $[ih]$ under the translation $\overrightarrow{je}$.

Question 2

(a)

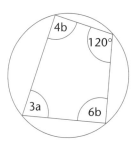

Evaluate a and b.

(b)

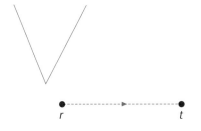

Construct the image of V under the translation $\overrightarrow{rt}$.

(c)

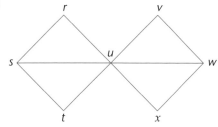

Find the image of:

(i) $\triangle sru$ under S_u, a central symmetry in the point u.

(ii) $\triangle uwx$ under $S_{[uw]}$, an axial symmetry in the line $[uw]$.

(iii) $[sr]$ under the translation $\overrightarrow{tx}$.

Question 3

(a) Construct the image of F under S_L, an axial symmetry in L.

(b)

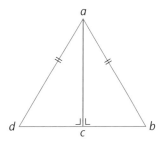

Explain why $\triangle abc$ and $\triangle adc$ are congruent.

(c)

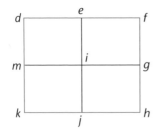

Find the image of:

(i) *mdei* under *Si*, a central symmetry in point *i*.

(ii) *mijk* under the translation $\overrightarrow{gf}$.

(iii) *ighj* under $S_{[ij]}$, an axial symmetry in the line [*ij*].

Solution to question 1

(a)

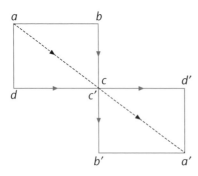

> **The image of □*abcd* under a central symmetry in the point *c*.**
>
> Draw a line from each point, through pt. c and out again the same distance. It is not necessary to name points *a'*, *b'*, *c'*, *d'*.

(b)

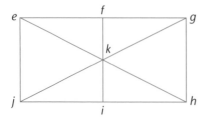

> **(i) Find the image of △*kgh* under S_k, a central symmetry in point *k*.**

Under S_k, $\qquad k \rightarrow k$

$\qquad\qquad\qquad\quad g \rightarrow j$

$\qquad\qquad\qquad\quad h \rightarrow e$

$\Rightarrow$ Image of △*kgh* under S_k is △*kje*

> **(ii) Find the image of [*ej*] under $S_{[fi]}$, an axial symmetry in the line [*fi*].**

Under $S_{[fi]}$, $\qquad e \rightarrow g$

$\qquad\qquad\qquad\quad\ j \rightarrow h$

$\Rightarrow$ Image of [*ej*] under $S_{[fi]}$ is [*gh*]

> **(iii) Find the image of [*ih*] under the translation $\overrightarrow{je}$.**

Under $\overrightarrow{je}$, $\qquad i \rightarrow f$

$\qquad\qquad\qquad\quad h \rightarrow g$

$\Rightarrow$ Image of [*ih*] under the translation $\overrightarrow{je}$ is [*fg*]

Solution to question 2

(a)

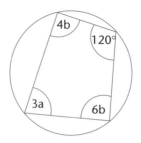

> **Evaluate *a* and *b*.**

$$4b + 6b = 180°$$

$$10b = 180°$$

$$\Rightarrow \qquad b = 18°$$

$$3a + 120° = 180°$$
$$3a = 180° - 120°$$
$$3a = 60° \quad \Rightarrow \underline{a = 20°}$$

(b)

> Construct the image of *V* under the translation $\overrightarrow{rt}$.

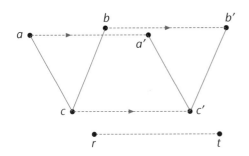

(c)

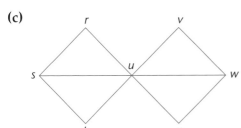

(i) Find the image of $\triangle sru$ under Su, a central symmetry in the point *u*.

Under Su,
$$s \rightarrow w$$
$$r \rightarrow x$$
$$u \rightarrow u$$

$\Rightarrow$ The image of $\triangle sru$ is $\underline{\triangle wxu}$

(ii) Find the image of $\triangle uwx$ under $S_{[uw]}$, an axial symmetry in the line $[uw]$.

Under $S_{[uw]}$,
$$u \rightarrow u$$
$$w \rightarrow w$$
$$x \rightarrow v$$

$\Rightarrow$ The image of $\triangle uwx$ is $\underline{\triangle uwv}$

(iii) Find the image of $[sr]$ under the translation $\overrightarrow{tx}$.

Under $\overrightarrow{tx}$,
$$s \rightarrow u$$
$$r \rightarrow v$$

$\Rightarrow$ The image of $[sr]$ is $\underline{[uv]}$

Solution to question 3

(a) Construct the image of *F* under an axial symmetry in the line *L*.

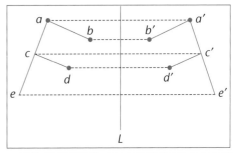

(b) Explain why $\triangle abc$ and $\triangle adc$ are congruent.

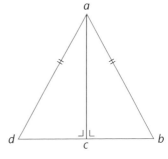

① *Investigate if the triangles have any angles which are equal.*

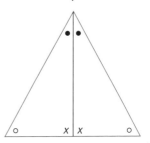

97

$(x) = (x)$ ... both 90°

$(\circ) = (\circ)$ ... because $|ad| = |ab|$

$(\bullet) = (\bullet)$ ... if 2 pairs of angles are equal, the third pair must be equal.

② *Investigate if the triangles have any sides which are equal.*

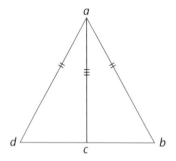

$|ab| = |ad|$ ... we are told this

$|ac| = |ac|$ ... same line

③ *Show the triangles are congruent.*

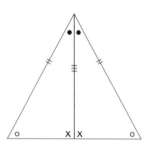

Therefore the triangles *are* congruent because of *SAS* (or *AAS* or *RHS*).

(c)

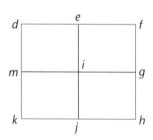

(i) Find the image of *mdei* under *Si*, a central symmetry in point *i*.

Under *Si*, $m \rightarrow g$

$d \rightarrow h$

$e \rightarrow j$

$i \rightarrow i$

$\Rightarrow$ The image of *mdei* is *ghji*

(ii) Find the image of *mijk* under the translation $\overrightarrow{gf}$.

Under $\overrightarrow{gf}$, $m \rightarrow d$

$i \rightarrow e$

$j \rightarrow i$

$k \rightarrow m$

$\Rightarrow$ The image of *mijk* is *deim*

(iii) Find the image of *ighj*, under $S_{[ij]}$ an axial symmetry in [*ij*].

Under $S_{[ij]}$, $i \rightarrow i$

$g \rightarrow m$

$h \rightarrow k$

$j \rightarrow j$

$\Rightarrow$ The image of *ighj* is *imkj*

Chapter **10**

Statistics

Section A
Mean and Mode of a List of Numbers

Type 1

Calculate the mean and mode of 2, 3, 4, 2, 6, 7.

Mean

Important

The 'mean' of a list of numbers is the 'average' of the list.

$\Rightarrow$ Mean $= \dfrac{2 + 3 + 4 + 2 + 6 + 7}{6}$

(We divide by 6 because the list contains 6 numbers.)

$$= \dfrac{24}{6} = 4$$

So, the mean of the list is 4.

Mode

Important

The 'mode' of a list of numbers is the number which occurs most often.

Therefore the mode of 2, 3, 4, 2, 6, 7 is 2 because it occurs more often than any of the other numbers.

Type 2

The mean of 1, x, 4, 5 is 3. Calculate x.

Method 1

We know from Type 1 that the mean of the above list is

$$\dfrac{1 + x + 4 + 5}{4}$$

$\Rightarrow \qquad \dfrac{1 + x + 4 + 5}{4} = 3$

$\Rightarrow \qquad \dfrac{10 + x}{4} = 3$

Write both sides as a fraction and cross-multiply.

$\Rightarrow \qquad \dfrac{10 + x}{4} = \dfrac{3}{1}$

Cross multiply ... $(10 + x)(1) = (3)(4)$

$\Rightarrow \qquad 10 + x = 12$

$\qquad\qquad x = 12 - 10$

$\Rightarrow \qquad \underline{x = 2}$

Method 2

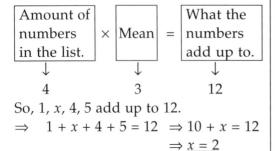

$$\underset{\downarrow}{\boxed{\begin{array}{c}\text{Amount of} \\ \text{numbers} \\ \text{in the list.}\end{array}}} \times \underset{\downarrow}{\boxed{\text{Mean}}} = \underset{\downarrow}{\boxed{\begin{array}{c}\text{What the} \\ \text{numbers} \\ \text{add up to.}\end{array}}}$$

$$\quad\ \ 4 \qquad\qquad 3 \qquad\qquad 12$$

So, 1, x, 4, 5 add up to 12.

$\Rightarrow\quad 1 + x + 4 + 5 = 12 \Rightarrow 10 + x = 12$

$\Rightarrow \underline{x = 2}$

Section B
Mean and Mode of a Frequency Distribution Table

A class of 20 pupils were given a multi-choice exam. The result of each pupil is given below:

3, 2, 5, 7, 2, 6, 4, 5, 1, 8, 8, 7, 4, 5, 6, 3, 2, 8, 8, 6.

(i) Represent the information above by means of a frequency distribution table.

(ii) Calculate the mean mark.

(iii) Calculate the modal mark

(i) *Draw a frequency table.*

Result in exam	1	2	3	4	5	6	7	8
Number of pupils	1	3	2	2	3	3	2	4

(ii) *Calculate the mean mark.*

Important

The mean of the frequency distribution table

Variable	a	b	c
Frequency	d	e	f

is found as follows:

$$\text{Mean} = \frac{(a \times d) + (b \times e) + (c \times f)}{d + e + f}$$

$\Rightarrow\quad$ Mean mark

$$= \frac{\begin{array}{c}(1 \times 1) + (2 \times 3) + (3 \times 2) + (4 \times 2) \\ + (5 \times 3) + (6 \times 3) + (7 \times 2) + (8 \times 4)\end{array}}{1 + 3 + 2 + 2 + 3 + 3 + 2 + 4}$$

$$= \frac{1 + 6 + 6 + 8 + 15 + 18 + 14 + 32}{1 + 3 + 2 + 2 + 3 + 3 + 2 + 4}$$

$$= \frac{100}{20} = 5 \Rightarrow \text{The mean is } \underline{5 \text{ marks}}.$$

(iii) *Calculate the modal mark.*

Important

The 'mode' (or modal mark) is the mark which occurs most often, i.e. the mark which has the highest frequency.

Mode ←

Result in exam	1	2	3	4	5	6	7	8
Number of pupils	1	3	2	2	3	3	2	4

Highest frequency ◄

Therefore, the modal mark is 8, as it has the highest frequency.

Please note from the above that the mode will *always* occur on the *top* row of a frequency table.

Section C
Pie Charts

Type 1

Favourite team	Liverpool	Celtic	Arsenal	Rangers
Number of people	4	12	6	2

The table above shows the number of people who follow various soccer teams. Represent the table above by means of a pie chart.

> **Important**
>
> Angle representing Liverpool
> $$= \frac{\text{Number who like Liverpool}}{\text{Total number}} \times \frac{360°}{1}$$

Liverpool
$$= \frac{4}{24} \times \frac{360°}{1} = 60°$$

Celtic
$$= \frac{12}{24} \times \frac{360°}{1} = 180°$$

Arsenal
$$= \frac{6}{24} \times \frac{360°}{1} = 90°$$

Rangers
$$\frac{2}{24} \times \frac{360°}{1} = 30°$$

> Check
>
> $60° + 180° + 90° + 30° = 360°$ ✓
>
> All answers must *always* add up to 360°.

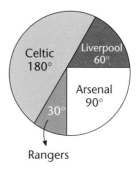

Type 2

The pie chart below shows the proportion of children who consider Mars, Twix, Moro or Snickers as their favourite chocolate bar.

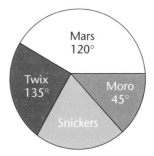

If there were 72 kids surveyed in total, calculate the number who liked each type of bar.

> **Important**
>
> Number who prefer Mars
> $$= \frac{\text{Angle representing Mars}}{\text{Total angle (always 360°)}} \times \frac{72}{1}$$
>
> (72 being the total number of people)

Mars
$$= \frac{120°}{360°} \times \frac{72}{1} = 24 \text{ people}$$

Moro

$$= \frac{45°}{360°} \times \frac{72}{1} = 9 \text{ people}$$

Twix

$$= \frac{135°}{360°} \times \frac{72}{1} = 27 \text{ people}$$

Snickers

> **Note**
>
> We do not know the angle representing Snickers.
>
> There are 360° in a full circle.
>
>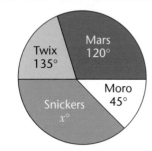
>
> $\Rightarrow \quad 120° + 45° + 135° + x° = 360°$
>
> $\Rightarrow \qquad\qquad 300° + x° = 360°$
>
> $\Rightarrow \qquad\qquad\qquad \underline{x° = 60°}$

$$= \frac{60°}{360°} \times \frac{72}{1} = 12 \text{ people}$$

> **Check**
>
> $\qquad 24 + 9 + 27 + 12 = 72 \checkmark$
>
> This is correct as the total number of people *is* 72.

Type 3

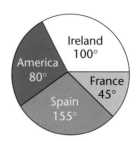

The pie chart above shows the holiday destinations of a group of people. If 16 people travelled to America, calculate how many went to the other destinations.

> **Important**
>
> '16 people travelled to America'
>
> $\Rightarrow \qquad 16 \text{ people} = 80°$
>
> *Divide both sides by 16*
>
> $\Rightarrow \qquad 1 \text{ person} = 5°$

Ireland

$$\times 20 \overbrace{\begin{array}{c} 1 \text{ person} = 5° \\ ? \text{ people} = 100° \end{array}} \times 20$$

$\Rightarrow \quad \underline{20 \text{ people}}$ travelled to Ireland.

Spain

$$\begin{array}{c} 1 \text{ person} = 5° \\ \times 31\downarrow \qquad\qquad \downarrow \times 31 \\ ? \text{ people} = 155° \end{array}$$

$\Rightarrow \quad \underline{31 \text{ people}}$ travelled to Spain.

France

$$\begin{array}{c} 1 \text{ person} = 5° \\ \times 9\downarrow \qquad\qquad \downarrow \times 9 \\ ? \text{ people} = 45° \end{array}$$

$\Rightarrow \quad \underline{9 \text{ people}}$ travelled to France.

Section D
Bar Charts

Represent the frequency table below by means of a bar chart:

Favourite drink	Fanta	Coca-Cola	Sprite	7UP
Number of people	5	7	3	1

Important

Remember that the *top* row of the table always goes on the *horizontal* axis.

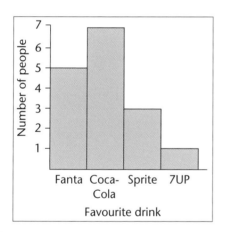

Please remember that you must *always* name each axis.

Section E
Trend Graphs

Use a trend graph to represent this frequency distribution table.

Month	Jan	Feb	March	April
cm of rain	10	17	12	4

The table shows the amount of rain (measured in cm) which fell in the first four months of the year.

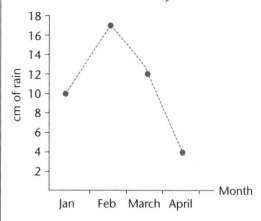

Chapter 10
Sample questions for you to try

Question 1

(a) The ages of 15 people were recorded as follows 14, 15, 13, 13, 15, 16, 15, 12, 15, 12, 16, 13, 14, 12, 15.

(i) Using a frequency distribution table, illustrate the above data.

(ii) Calculate the mean age of the group.

(iii) Calculate the modal age.

(b) (i) Illustrate the frequency table from part (a) by means of a bar chart.

(ii) Calculate the percentage of people who were 15 years or older.

Question 2

(a) (i) The mean of 4, 2, 1, *a*, 6 is 3. Calculate *a*.

(ii) Hence find the mode.

(b) The methods by which 24 students travel to school are shown below:

Travel method	Walk	Car	Bus	Bicycle
Number of pupils	5	7	10	2

Illustrate the information above using a pie chart. Check your answer.

(c) The number of ice creams sold in a particular shop is shown below:

Month	May	June	July	Aug.	Sept.
Number sold	80	100	200	180	90

(i) Construct a trend graph to represent the table.

(ii) What does the trend graph tell us about the weather during the summer months that year?

(iii) Calculate the fraction of total ice cream sold in June in its simplest form.

Question 3

(a)

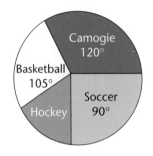

Camogie 120°
Basketball 105°
Soccer 90°
Hockey

The pie chart shows the favourite sports of a class of girls. If 6 girls like

soccer, calculate how many like the other sports.

(b) Calculate the mean and mode of 4, 2, 6, 3, 2, 1.

(c)

Money received	5	8	10	12	15
Number of kids	4	3	5	6	2

This frequency table shows the pocket money received (in €) by a group of children.

(i) Calculate the mean amount of money received (to the nearest euro).

(ii) What is the modal amount of pocket money?

(iii) Calculate the percentage of children who received less than €9.

Solution to question 1

(a) Given the ages 14, 15, 13, 13, 15, 16, 15, 12, 15, 12, 16, 13, 14, 12, 15.

(i) Illustrate the information using a frequency table.

Age in years	12	13	14	15	16
Number of kids	3	3	2	5	2

(ii) Calculate the mean age.

$$\text{Mean} = \frac{(12 \times 3) + (13 \times 3) + (14 \times 2) + (15 \times 5) + (16 \times 2)}{3 + 3 + 2 + 5 + 2}$$

$$= \frac{36 + 39 + 28 + 75 + 32}{3 + 3 + 2 + 5 + 2}$$

$$= \frac{210}{15} = 14$$

⇒   Mean age is 14 years.

(iii) Calculate the modal age.

Mode

Age	12	13	14	15	16
Number	3	3	2	5	2

Highest frequency

Therefore, the mode is 15 years as it has the highest frequency.

(b)

(i) Illustrate the frequency table by means of a bar chart.

Age in years	12	13	14	15	16
Number of kids	3	3	2	5	2

⇓

Remember

① *Top* row of table goes on the *horizontal* row of the chart.

② **Name both axes clearly.**

⇓

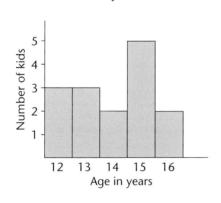

(ii) Calculate the percentage of kids who were 15 years or older.

Important

$$\% \ 15 \text{ or older} = \frac{\text{Number who are 15 or older}}{\text{Total number}} \times \frac{100}{1}$$

$$= \frac{7}{15} \times \frac{100}{1} = 46.67\%$$

Solution to question 2

(a)

(i) The mean of 4, 2, 1, a, 6 is 3. Find a.

Either of the following methods is fine:

Method 1

Mean of 4, 2, 1, a, 6

is $\qquad \dfrac{4 + 2 + 1 + a + 6}{5}$

⇒ $\qquad \dfrac{4 + 2 + 1 + a + 6}{5} = 3$

⇒ $\qquad \dfrac{13 + a}{5} = \dfrac{3}{1}$

Cross multiply … $(13 + a)(1) = (3)(5)$

⇒ $\qquad 13 + a = 15$

⇒ $\qquad \underline{a = 2}$

Method 2

Amount of numbers in the list	×	Mean	=	What the numbers add up to
↓		↓		↓
5		3	=	15

So, 4, 2, 1, a, 6 add up to 15.

⇒ $\qquad 4 + 2 + 1 + a + 6 = 15$

$\Rightarrow$ $\qquad$ $13 + a = 15$

$\Rightarrow$ $\qquad$ $a = 2$

(ii) Find the mode.

As $a = 2$, the list is 4, 2, 1, 2, 6.

$\Rightarrow$ Mode = 2 as it occurs most often.

(b)

Travel method	Walk	Car	Bus	Bike
Number of pupils	5	7	10	2

Illustrate the table by means of a pie chart.

Walk

$$\frac{\text{Number who walk}}{\text{Total number}} \times \frac{360°}{1}$$

$$= \frac{5}{24} \times \frac{360°}{1} = \boxed{75°}$$

Car

$$\frac{7}{24} \times \frac{360°}{1} = \boxed{105°}$$

Bus

$$\frac{10}{24} \times \frac{360°}{1} = \boxed{150°}$$

Bicycle

$$\frac{2}{24} \times \frac{360°}{1} = \boxed{30°}$$

Check

$$75° + 105° + 150° + 30° = 360° ✓$$

(c)

Month	May	June	July	Aug.	Sept.
Number sold	80	100	200	180	90

(i) Illustrate the above table using a trend graph.

Number sold

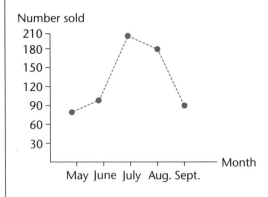

(ii) What does the trend graph tell us about the weather during the summer months?

Because there was a sharp increase in the amount of ice cream sold during July and August in particular, this would suggest that the weather during these months was very warm.

(iii) What fraction of the total amount of ice cream is sold in June?

Amount sold in June = 100

Total amount is

$$80 + 100 + 200 + 180 + 90 = 650$$

$\Rightarrow$ $\qquad$ $\dfrac{100}{650}$

$$[\div 5] = \frac{20}{130}$$

$$[\div 10] = \left(\frac{2}{13}\right)$$

Solution to question 3

(a)

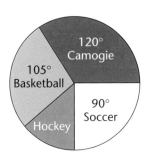

6 girls like soccer. Find how many like the other 3 sports.

Important

'6 girls like soccer'

$\Rightarrow$ 6 girls = 90°

($\div$ 6) So, 1 girl = 15°.*

Basketball

         1 girl = 15°

$\times 7$ $\downarrow$ $\downarrow$ [$\times$ 7]

         7 girls = 105°

So 7 girls like basketball.

Camogie

         1 girl = 15°

$\times 8$ $\downarrow$ [$\times$ 8]

         8 girls = 120°

So, 8 girls like camogie.

Hockey

Angle representing hockey

= 360° − (105° + 120° + 90°)

= 360° − 315°

= 45°

         1 girl = 15°

$\times 3$ $\downarrow$ $\downarrow$ [$\times$ 3]

         3 girls = 45°

So, 3 girls like hockey.

(b) Calculate the mean and mode of 4, 2, 6, 3, 2, 1.

Mean $= \dfrac{4 + 2 + 6 + 3 + 2 + 1}{6}$

$= \dfrac{18}{6} = \boxed{3}$

Mode = 2 as it occurs most often.

(c)

Money received (€)	5	8	10	12	15
Number of kids	4	3	5	6	2

(i) Calculate the mean amount received (to the nearest euro).

Mean $= \dfrac{\begin{array}{c}(5 \times 4) + (8 \times 3) + (10 \times 5) \\ + (12 \times 6) + (15 \times 2)\end{array}}{4 + 3 + 5 + 6 = 2}$

$= \dfrac{20 + 24 + 50 + 72 + 30}{4 + 3 + 5 + 6 + 2}$

$= \dfrac{196}{20} = 9.8$

So, the mean amount received is €10, to the nearest euro.

(ii) What is the modal amount of pocket money?

Mode

Money received	5	8	10	12	15
Number of kids	4	3	5	6	2

Highest frequency

$\Rightarrow$ €12 is the modal amount.

(iii) Calculate the percentage of pupils who received less than €9.

$$\frac{\text{Number who received less than } €9}{\text{Total number}} \times \frac{100}{1}$$

$$\Rightarrow \qquad \frac{7}{20} \times \frac{100}{1} = \underline{35\%}$$

Chapter 11
Angles and Constructions

Section A
Angles

Note 1

'A straight angle is equal to 180°.'

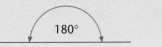

Example

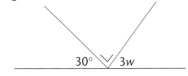

$\Rightarrow$ $30° + 90° + 3w = 180°$ . . . straight angle

$\Rightarrow$ $120° + 3w = 180°$

             $3w = 180° - 120°$

$\Rightarrow$ $3w = 60°$

$\Rightarrow$ $\underline{w = 20°}$

Note 2

'Vertically opposite angles are equal.'

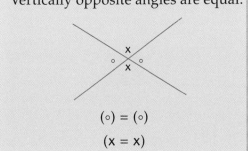

$(\circ) = (\circ)$

$(x = x)$

Example

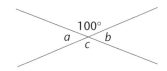

Evaluate *a*, *b* and *c*.

$\Rightarrow$ ① $\underline{c = 100°}$ . . . the angles are vertically opposite

② $100 + b = 180°$ . . . straight angle

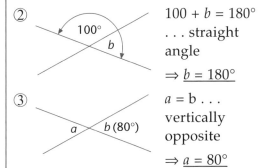

$\Rightarrow \underline{b = 180°}$

③ $a = b$ . . . vertically opposite

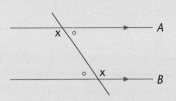

$\Rightarrow \underline{a = 80°}$

Note 3

In the diagram A // B

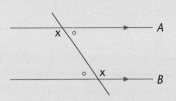

$(x) = (x)$ and $(\circ) = (\circ)$

These angles are equal because they are <u>alternate</u> angles.

This *only* occurs because line *A* and line *B* are *parallel*.

Example

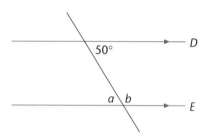

In the given diagram
D // E.

Evaluate a and b.

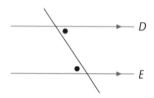

$a = 50°$ . . . alternate angles

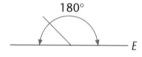

$a + b = 180°$ . . . straight angle

$\Rightarrow$ $50° + b = 180°$

$\Rightarrow$ $b = 180° - 50°$ $b = 130°$

Note 4

In the diagram F // G

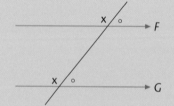

(x) = (x) and (∘) = (∘) because these are <u>corresponding</u> angles.

This *only* occurs when line *f* and line *g* are *parallel*.

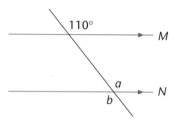

$\Rightarrow$ In the diagram M // N calculate a and b.

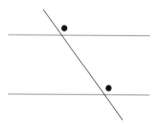

$a = 110°$ . . . corresponding angles

$a = b$ . . . vertically opposite

$\Rightarrow$ $b = 110°$

Section B
Triangles

Type 1
Right-angled triangles

Note 1

'If a triangle is right-angled, its area is $^1/_2$ (base) × (perpendicular height)'

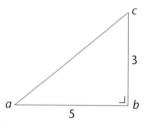

① [ab] is perpendicular to [bc] because the angle between them is 90°.

② Therefore area $\triangle abc$

$$= \frac{1}{2} (5) \times (3) = \underline{7.5}$$

Note 2

'Theory of Pythagoras'

(Hypotenuse)^2 = (side 1)^2 + (side 2)^2

① The 'Hypotenuse' is the side opposite the 90° angle.

② We use the theory of Pythagoras when:

   (a) The triangle is right-angled.

   (b) We have the length of two sides and we wish to find the third side.

Example 1

Find x

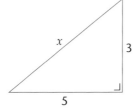

x is the hypotenuse so it is written first.

$\Rightarrow \quad x^2 = 3^2 + 5^2$

$\quad\quad x^2 = 9 + 25$

$\Rightarrow \quad x^2 = 34$

$\quad\quad \underline{x = \sqrt{34}}$

Example 2

Find x

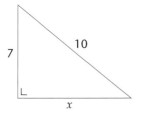

Important

Here 10 is the hypotenuse so *it* is written first.

$\Rightarrow \quad\quad\quad\quad 10^2 = 7^2 + x^2$

$\Rightarrow \quad\quad\quad\quad 100 = 49 + x^2$

$\quad\quad\quad\quad\quad 100 - 49 = x^2$

$\quad\quad 51 = x^2 \quad \Rightarrow \underline{\sqrt{51} = x}$

Type 2
Isosceles triangles

Note 1

A triangle is 'isosceles' if any *two* of its sides are equal in length.

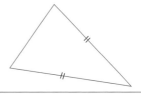

Note 2

When two sides of a triangle are equal, the angles opposite these sides are also equal in measure.

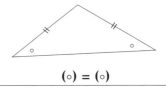

$$(\circ) = (\circ)$$

Example 1

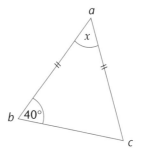

In $\triangle abc$ $|ab| = |ac|$ and $|\angle abc| =$ 40°. Evaluate $|\angle bac|$

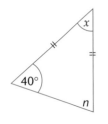 $\Rightarrow$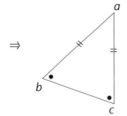

Because $\qquad |ab| = |ac|$

$$(\bullet) = (\bullet)$$

$\Rightarrow \qquad\qquad n = 40°$

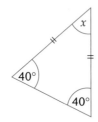

$$40° + 40° + x = 180°$$

$\Rightarrow \qquad\qquad 80° + x = 180°$

$$x = 100°$$

$\Rightarrow \qquad\qquad |\angle bac| = 100°$

Example 2

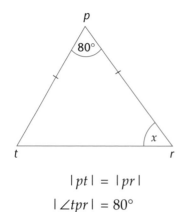

$$|pt| = |pr|$$

$$|\angle tpr| = 80°$$

Evaluate $|\angle trp|$

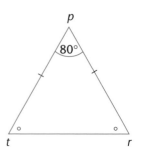

$$|pt| = |pr|$$

$\Rightarrow \qquad\qquad (\circ) = (\circ)$

$$80° + (\circ) + (\circ) = 180°$$

$\Rightarrow \qquad\qquad 80° + 2(\circ) = 180°$

$$2(\circ) = 180° - 80°$$

$$2(\circ) = 100°$$

$\Rightarrow \qquad\qquad (\circ) = 50°$

$\Rightarrow \qquad\qquad |\angle |ptr| = 50°$

Section C
Parallelograms

Note 1

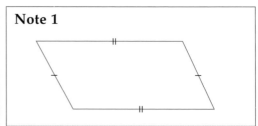

'The opposite sides of a parallelogram are equal in measure.'

Note 2

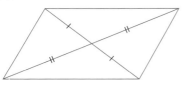

'The diagonals of a parallelogram bisect each other.'

(They cut each other into two equal parts.)

Note 3

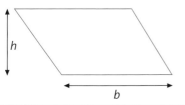

The area of a parallelogram is:
(base) × (perpendicular height)

$\Rightarrow$ $\quad$ $\underline{\text{Area} = b \times h}$

⇓

Example

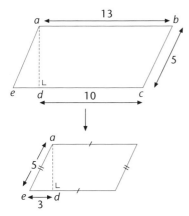

↓

Given the diagram above, find $|ad|$. Also, find the area of *abce*.

Evaluate $|ad|$

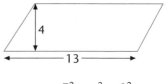

$$5^2 = x^2 + 3^2$$
$$25 = x^2 + 9$$
$$25 - 9 = x^2$$
$$16 = x^2$$
$\Rightarrow$ $\qquad\qquad$ $4 = x$

Area = $13 \times 4 = 52$

Note 4

In any parallelogram, opposite angles are equal.

$\Rightarrow$ $\qquad$ $(\circ) = (\circ)$ and $(x) = (x)$

Also, $\qquad$ $(\circ) + (x) = 180°$

⇓

Evaluate a, b, c.

$\underline{a = 50°}$ . . . opposite angles in a parallelogram

Also, $\qquad\qquad$ $a + b = 180°$
$$50° + b = 180$$
$\Rightarrow$ $\qquad\qquad\qquad$ $\underline{b = 130°}$

Also, $\qquad\qquad$ $a + c = 180°$
$$50° + c = 180°$$
$\Rightarrow$ $\qquad\qquad\qquad$ $\underline{c = 130°}$

Note 5

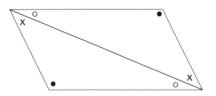

In any parallelogram,

(x) = (x) ... alternate angles

(○) = (○) ... alternate angles

(•) = (•) ... opposite angles in a parallelogram

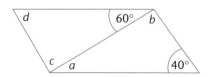

Evaluate a, b, c, d.

$d = 40°$ ... opposite angles in a parallelogram

$a = 60°$ ... alternate angles

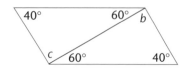

$\Rightarrow \qquad 60° + b + 40° = 180°$

$\qquad \qquad 100° + b = 180°$

$\Rightarrow \qquad \qquad b = 180° - 100°$

$\qquad \qquad \underline{b = 80°}$

$b = c$ ... alternate angles

$\Rightarrow \qquad \qquad \underline{c = 80°}$

Section D
Angle in a Semicircle

Note 1

* It is *very* important that you understand the following.

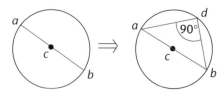

In the diag. above *please* understand that [ab] is a *diameter* of the circle.

It is a diameter because it passes through the centre of the circle.

∠adb starts at one end of the diameter and finishes at the other end.

Any angle which does this is 90°.

∠adb is said to be an 'angle in a semicircle'.

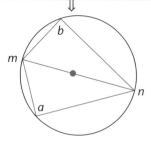

Here, $a = 90°$ and $b = 90°$ because both angles start and finish at the end points of the diameter [mn].

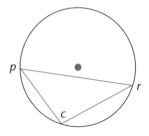

Here $c \neq 90°$ because $[pr]$ is *not* a diameter.

Example 1

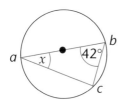

$$|\angle abc| = 42°$$

Calculate $|\angle cab|$.

$|\angle acb| = 90°$ . . . angle in a semicircle

$\Rightarrow \qquad x + 42° + 90° = 180°$

$\qquad\qquad x + 132° = 180°$

$\qquad\qquad\qquad x = 48°$

$\Rightarrow \qquad \underline{|\angle cab| = 48°}$

Example 2

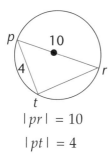

$$|pr| = 10$$
$$|pt| = 4$$

Find $|rt|$.

* $|\angle ptr| = 90°$ . . . angle in a semicircle

$\Rightarrow \quad \triangle ptr$ is right-angled

So, we can use the theory of Pythagorus . . .

$$10^2 = 4^2 + x^2$$
$$100 = 16 + x^2$$
$$100 - 16 = x^2$$
$$84 = x^2$$

$\Rightarrow \qquad \underline{\sqrt{84} = x}$

Example 3

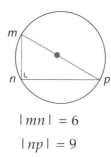

$$|mn| = 6$$
$$|np| = 9$$

Find the area $\triangle mnp$.

$\qquad * |\angle mnp| = 90°$

$\Rightarrow \qquad [mn] \perp [np]$

Area $= \dfrac{1}{2}$ (base) $\times$ (perpendicular height)

$\qquad = \dfrac{1}{2}(6)(9) = \textcircled{27}$

Note 2

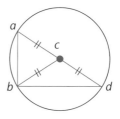

In the given diagram, $|ac| = |bc| = |cd|$ as each line is a radius of the circle.

***Please get into the habit of marking in all radii in diagrams such as this.**

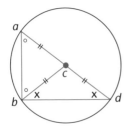

① △*abc* is an isosceles triangle.
Because | *ac* | = | *bc* | then (○) = (○).

② △*bcd* is an isosceles triangle.
Because | *bc* | = | *cd* | then (x) =
(x).

⇓

Example (*very* important)

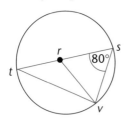

In the diagram, | ∠*rsv* | = 80°.

Calculate the measure of all other
angles.

Step 1

$$(\circ) = (\circ)$$
$$(x) = (x)$$

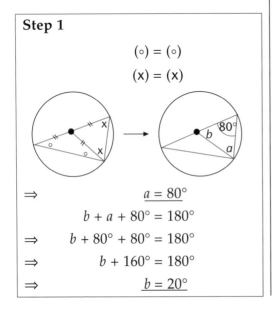

⇒ $\underline{a = 80°}$

$b + a + 80° = 180°$

⇒ $b + 80° + 80° = 180°$

⇒ $b + 160° = 180°$

⇒ $\underline{b = 20°}$

Step 2

(○) + (x) = 90° (angle in a semicircle)

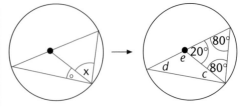

① ⇒ $c + 80° = 90°$ ⇒ $\underline{c = 10°}$

② $c = d$ ⇒ $\underline{d = 10°}$

③ $e + c + d = 180°$

⇒ $e + 10° + 10° = 180°$

⇒ $\underline{e = 160°}$

Section E
Constructions

There are only 4 different
constructions which we have to know.

They are quite easy but please
remember:

① All construction lines should be
drawn in pencil.

② Construction lines account for a
lot of marks so show them clearly.

Construction 1

Construct the perpendicular
bisector of the line [*ab*].

① Place the compass on point *a*.
Extend so that the compass is
greater than half the length of [*ab*].

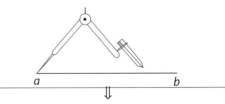

⇓

② With the compass on pt. *a* draw an arc above and below the line.

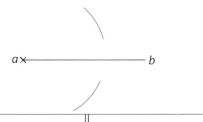

③ Place the compass as pt. *b*. Again, swing an arc above and below the line.

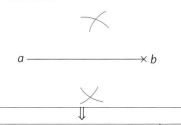

④ Draw a line joining the points where the arcs meet.

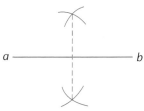

This line is the perpendicular bisector of [*ab*].

Construction 2

Construct the bisector of ∠*abc*.

① Place the compass at point *b*. Swing an arc as shown.

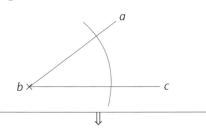

② Place the compass on point ⓘ and swing an arc.

With the compass on point ⓘⓘ swing another arc.

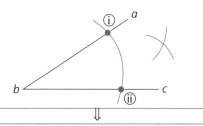

③ Join the point of intersection of both arcs to point *b*.

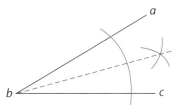

This line is the bisector of ∠*abc*.

Construction 3

Divide [*ab*] into 4 equal parts.

① Draw a line from pt. *a* as shown.

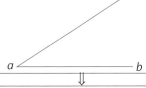

② Using the compass, draw 4 arcs along the line such that |*ac*| = |*cd*| = |*de*| = |*ef*|.

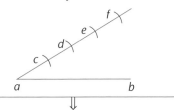

③ Join *f* to *b*. Draw parallel lines from pts. *e*, *d* and *c*.

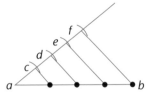

Hence [*ab*] is divided into 4 equal parts.

Construction 4

Constructing triangles

There are three types of question which can be asked here. Please read through and understand the steps in each type.

Type 1

Construct △*abc* such that |*ab*| = 4 cm, |*bc*| = 6 cm and |*ac*| = 5 cm.

① Draw a rough diagram of what △*abc* should look like.

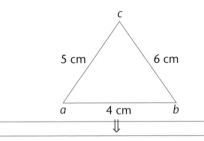

② Draw [*ab*] 4 cm in length.

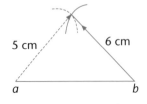

Put the compass on pt. *a*. Draw an arc 5 cm fom *a*. Put the compass on pt. *b*. Draw an arc 6 cm from *b*.

⇓

③ Pt. *c* is the point where the arcs meet.

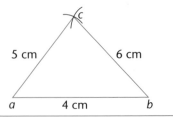

Type 2

Construct △*mnp* such that |*mn*| = 6 cm, |*np*| = 7 cm and |∠*mnp*| = 72°.

① Draw a rough diagram.

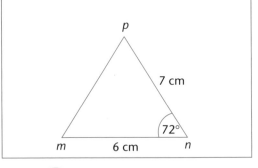

Because *n* is the middle letter, ∠*mnp* is at point *n*.

② Draw [*mn*].

* We pick this line because it includes point *n*.

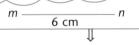

⇓

118

③ At pt. *n*, use a protractor to measure an angle of 72°. Draw a line to show the angle.

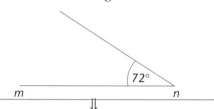

④ From pt. *n* draw an arc 7 cm.

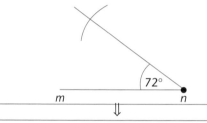

⑤ Point *p* is where the arc and the construction line intersect.

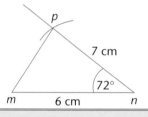

Type 3

Construct △*mpt* such that |*mp*| = 5 cm, |∠*mpt*| = 80° and |∠*pmt*| = 50°.

① Draw a rough sketch of what △*mpt* should look like.

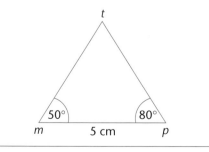

② Draw [*mp*].

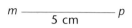

③ With your protractor measure 80° from point *p* (as |∠*mpt* = 80°).

Measure 50° from point *m* (as |∠*pmt*| = 50°).

Point *t* is where these two construction lines meet.

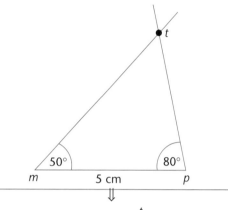

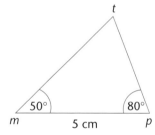

Chapter 11
Sample questions for you to try

Question 1

(a)

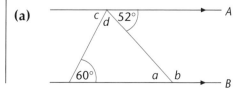

119

In the given diagram, $A \parallel B$.
Evaluate a, b, c and d.

(b) Construct $\triangle prt$ such that $|pr| = $ 10 cm, $|rt| = 7$ cm and $|tp| = 6$ cm.

(c)

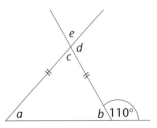

In the given diagram, evaluate a, b, c, d and e.

Question 2

(a)

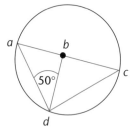

In the given diagram $|\angle bda| = 50°$ with b the centre of the circle.

(i) Name two isosceles triangles, giving a reason for your answer.

(ii) Evaluate (a) $|\angle bcd|$
　　　　　　 (b) $|\angle abd|$

(b) Copy the angle below. Using your compass, bisect the angle, showing all construction lines clearly.

(c)

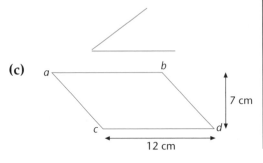

In the given diagram, $|cd| = 12$.
Calculate the area of the parallelogram.

Question 3

(a)

Draw a line $[mp]$ 7 cm in length.

Use your compass to divide the line into three equal parts. Show all construction lines clearly.

(b)

Evaluate a, b and c in the above parallelogram.

(c)

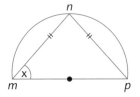

Here we see that $|mn| = |np|$.
Evaluate x.

Solution to question 1

(a)

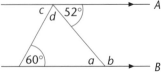

Evaluate a, b, c, d.

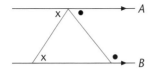

Because $A \parallel B$,

$(\times) = (\times)$

$(\bullet) = (\bullet)$

$\Rightarrow$ $\underline{a = 52°}$ and $\underline{c = 60°}$

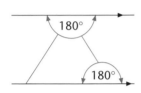

Both these angles are 180° . . . straight angles

$\Rightarrow$ $c + d + 52° = 180°$

$\qquad 60° + d + 52° = 180°$

$\qquad d + 112° = 180°$

$\Rightarrow \qquad \underline{d = 68°}$

$\qquad a + b = 180°$

$\qquad 52° + b = 180°$

$\Rightarrow \qquad \underline{b = 128°}$

(b) Construct $\triangle prt$ such that $|pr| = 10$ cm, $|rt| = 7$ cm and $|tp| = 6$ cm.

Rough diagram

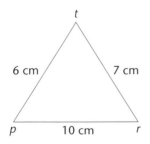

Construct the $\triangle prt$.

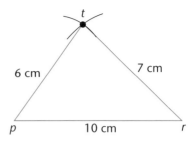

(c)

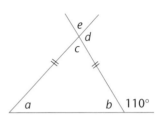

① $b + 110° = 180°$ . . . straight angle
$\underline{b = 70°}$

② The triangle is isosceles.
$\Rightarrow$ $a = b$ $\Rightarrow$ $\underline{a = 70°}$

③ $a + b + c = 180°$

$\Rightarrow 70° + 70° + c = 180°$

$\Rightarrow 140° + c = 180°$ $\Rightarrow$ $\underline{c = 40°}$

④ $c = e$ . . . vertically opposite

$\Rightarrow$ $\underline{e = 40°}$

⑤ $c + d = 180°$ . . . straight angle

$\Rightarrow 40° + d = 180°$ $\Rightarrow$ $\underline{d = 140°}$

Solution to question 2

(a)

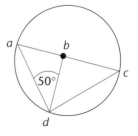

(i) Name, giving a reason, two isosceles triangles.

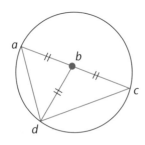

$|ab| = |bd| = |bc| \dots$ all radii

$\Rightarrow \quad \triangle abd$ is isosceles $(|ab| = |bd|)$

$\triangle bcd$ is isosceles $(|bd| = |bc|)$

(ii) Evaluate:

   (a) $|\angle bcd|$

   (b) $|\angle abd|$

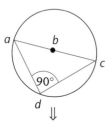 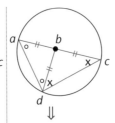

$|\angle adc| = 90$

$\Rightarrow |\angle bdc| + 50°$
$= 90°$

$\Rightarrow \underline{|\angle bdc| = 40°}$

$(\circ) = (\circ)$
$(\times) = (\times)$

$\Rightarrow |\angle bdc| = |\angle bcd|$

$\Rightarrow \underline{|\angle bcd| = 40°}$

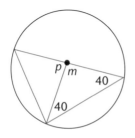

① $m + 40° + 40° = 180°$

     $m + 80° = 180°$

$\Rightarrow \quad m = 100°$

② $p + m = 180° \dots$ straight angle

$\Rightarrow \quad p + 100° = 180°$

So, $p = 80°$

$\Rightarrow \quad \underline{|\angle abd| = 80°}$

(b)

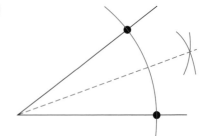

(c)

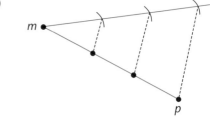

Area of parallelogram

    $= \text{base} \times \text{perpendicular height}$

    $= 12 \text{ cm} \times 7 \text{ cm} = \underline{84 \text{ cm}^2}$

Solution to question 3

(a)

(b)

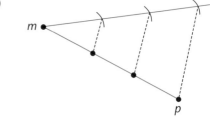

Evaluate a, b and c.

$(\circ) = (\circ)$

$(\times) = (\times)$

$$\Rightarrow \qquad 3a = 120°$$

$$a = \frac{120°}{3}$$

$$\Rightarrow \qquad \underline{a = 40°}$$

$$(\mathsf{x}) + (\circ) = 180°$$

① $\Rightarrow \qquad 3a + 2b = 180°$

$a = 40° \Rightarrow 3(40°) + 2b = 180°$

$$120° + 2b = 180°$$

$$2b = 180° - 120°$$

$$2b = 60° \quad \Rightarrow \quad \underline{b = 30°}$$

② $4c = 2b$

$b = 30° \quad \Rightarrow \quad 4c = 2(30°)$

$$4c = 60°$$

$$c = \frac{60°}{4}$$

$\Rightarrow \quad \underline{c = 15°}$

(c)

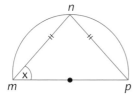

Evaluate x.

⇓

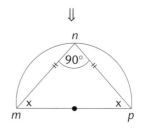

① $|\angle mnp| = 90°$ as $[mp]$ is a diameter.

② $(\mathsf{x}) = (\mathsf{x})$ as $|mn| = |np|$.

③ $(\mathsf{x}) + (\mathsf{x}) + 90° = 180°$

$$\Rightarrow \qquad (\mathsf{x}) + (\mathsf{x}) = 90°$$

$$\Rightarrow \qquad 2(\mathsf{x}) = 90°$$

$$\underline{\text{So, } \mathsf{x} = 45°}$$

Chapter **12**
Coordinate Geometry

Section A
Slope of a Line

Type 1

Given a (–2, 5), b (3, –2) find the slope of [ab].

> **Important**
> The slope between two points is
>
> given as: $\dfrac{y_2 - y_1}{x_2 - x_1}$

$$a(-2, 5) \qquad\qquad b(3, -2)$$
$$x_1\, y_1 \qquad\qquad\qquad x_2\, y_2$$

$$\text{Slope} = \frac{y_2 - y_1}{x_2 - x_1}$$

$$= \frac{-2 - 5}{3 - -2} = \frac{-2 - 5}{3 + 2}$$

$$= \frac{-7}{5}$$

$\Rightarrow$ Slope of [ab] is $\dfrac{-7}{5}$

Type 2

Find the slope of $3x + 2y - 1 = 0$

① **Isolate the y term on the left of the '=' sign.**

$\Rightarrow\ 2y = -3x + 1$

② **Divide across by the number before the y term.**

$\Rightarrow\ \dfrac{2}{2}y = \dfrac{-3}{2}x + \dfrac{1}{2}$

$\Rightarrow\ y = \dfrac{-3}{2}x + \dfrac{1}{2}$

③ **The slope of the line is the number before the x term.**

$\Rightarrow\qquad \text{Slope} = \dfrac{-3}{2}$

Section B
Midpoint

Given p(–3, 4), r(–7, –2), find point t, the midpoint of [pr].

> **Important**
>
> The midpoint of any two points is
>
> given as $\left(\dfrac{x_1 + x_2}{2},\ \dfrac{y_1 + y_2}{2} \right)$

$$p(-3, 4) \qquad\qquad r(-7, -2)$$
$$x_1\, y_1 \qquad\qquad\qquad x_2\, y_2$$

$$\text{Midpoint} = \left(\frac{x_1 + x_2}{2},\ \frac{y_1 + y_2}{2} \right)$$

$$= \left(\frac{-3 - 7}{2}, \frac{4 - 2}{2} \right) = \left(\frac{-10}{2}, \frac{2}{2} \right)$$

$\Rightarrow\qquad$ Midpoint of [pr] is <u>(–5, 1)</u>

Section C
Distance between Two Points

Given $g(-3, 5)$, $h(-8, -2)$ calculate $|gh|$, the distance between point g and point h.

> **Important**
>
> The distance between any two points is $\sqrt{(x_2 - x_1)^2 + (y_2 - y_1)^2}$

$$g(-3, 5) \qquad\qquad h(-8, -2)$$
$$\quad x_1\, y_1 \qquad\qquad\qquad x_2\, y_2$$

Distance $= \sqrt{(x_2 - x_1)^2 + (y_2 - y_1)^2}$

$\qquad\quad = \sqrt{(-8 - -3)^2 + (-2 - 5)^2}$

$\qquad\quad = \sqrt{(-8 + 3)^2 + (-2 - 5)^2}$

$\qquad\quad = \sqrt{(-5)^2 + (-7)^2}$

> **Note**
>
> When squaring a negative number be sure to first put the number in a bracket.
>
> **Example**
>
> $(-5)^2$
>
> *Sharp calculator*
>
> $\boxed{(\ \boxed{\pm}\ 5)\ \boxed{x^2}} = 25$
>
> *Casio calculator*
>
> $\boxed{(\ (-)\ 5)\ \boxed{x^2}}$

$\qquad\quad = \sqrt{25 + 49} = \sqrt{74}$

$\Rightarrow \quad |gh| = 8.6$

Section D
Point of Intersection

Type 1

Find the coordinates of point c, the point where $3x - 5y - 9 = 0$ cuts the x-axis.

> **Important**
>
> To find where a line cuts the x-axis, let y equal to 0.

$$3x - 5y - 9 = 0$$

Let $y = 0$

$\Rightarrow \qquad\qquad 3x - 5(0) - 9 = 0$

$\Rightarrow \qquad\qquad 3x - 0 - 9 = 0$

$\Rightarrow \qquad\qquad 3x = 9 \ \Rightarrow \ x = 3$

So, $x = 3$ and $y = 0$

$\Rightarrow \qquad\qquad\qquad \underline{c(3, 0)}$

Type 2

Given $L: 2x + 3y - 6 = 0$, find point d, the point of intersection of L and the y-axis.

> **Important**
>
> To find where a line cuts the y-axis, let x equal to 0.

$$2x + 3y - 6 = 0$$

Let $x = 0$

$$2(0) + 3y - 6 = 0$$

$\Rightarrow \qquad\qquad 0 + 3y - 6 = 0$

$$3y = 6 \ \Rightarrow y = 2$$

So, $x = 0$ and $y = 2$

Remember that in any point, the x value is *always* written first.

$\Rightarrow$ $\underline{d(0, 2)}$

Section E
Area of a Triangle

Type 1

Given $a(3, 0)$ $b(0, 8)$, find the area of the triangle abo, where o the origin.

Important

The 'origin' is the point $(0, 0)$.

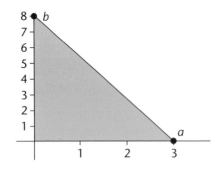

Area = $\frac{1}{2}$ (base) × (perpendicular height)

$= \frac{1}{2}$ (3) × 8

$= 12$

Type 2

Given $p(-2, 0)$, $r(6, 0)$ and $t(5, 3)$

(i) Plot all three points.

(ii) Calculate the area of the triangle prt.

(i)

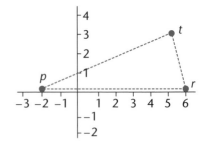

(ii) Area of a triangle = $\frac{1}{2}$ (base) × (perpendicular height)

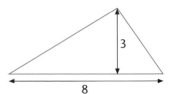

Please check the first diagram and understand clearly why the base is 8 units and why the perpendicular height is 3 units.

$\Rightarrow$ Area = $\frac{1}{2}$ (8) × (3)

$= 12$

Section F
Point on a Line

Type 1

Prove $(3, -4)$ is a point on the line $2x + 3y + 6 = 0$.

To show a point is on a line:

① Substitute the point into the equation of the line.

② If it's on the line it will *satisfy* the equation. (i.e. both sides of the '=' sign will be equal)

$$2x + 3y + 6 = 0$$

Fill in (3, –4)

$$2(3) + 3(-4) + 6 = 0$$
$$6 - 12 + 6 = 0$$
$$0 = 0 \checkmark$$

As (3, –4) satisfies the equation, it *is* on the line.

Type 2

If (2*t*, –4) is on the line $3x + 5y + 2 = 0$ evaluate *t*.

> Again, let $2t = x$ and let $-4 = y$.
> Because (2*t*, –4) is on the line it *does* satisfy the equation.

$$3x + 5y + 2 = 0$$

Fill in (2t, –4)

$$3(2t) + 5(-4) + 2 = 0$$
$$6t - 20 + 2 = 0$$
$$6t - 18 = 0$$
$$6t = 18$$
$$\Rightarrow \quad t = 3$$

Type 3

(2, –4) is on the line $5x + ty + 2 = 0$. Evaluate *t*.

$$5x + ty + 2 = 0$$

Fill in (2, –4)

$$5(2) + t(-4) + 2 = 0$$
$$\Rightarrow \quad 10 - 4t + 2 = 0$$
$$-4t + 12 = 0$$
$$-4t = -12$$
$$\Rightarrow \quad t = \frac{-12}{-4}$$
$$t = 3$$

Chapter 12
Sample questions for you to try

Question 1

(a) Given $a(-1, 4)$ and $b(5, -10)$

   (i) Find the coordinates of point *d*, the midpoint of [*ab*].

   (ii) Prove that distance $|ad|$ = distance $|bd|$.

(b) $P: 2x - 6y - 18 = 0$.

   (i) *P* cuts the *x*-axis at point *f*. Find the coordinates of point *f*.

   (ii) *P* intersects the *y*-axis at point *g*. Find the coordinates of point *g*.

   (iii) Find the slope of [*fg*].

   (iv) Find the equation of [*fg*].

Question 2

(a) Given $t(-2, 3)$ and $u(5, -1)$

   (i) Find the slope of [*tu*].

   (ii) Find the equation of [*tu*].

(b) $r(0, -4)$, $p(0, 3)$ and $w(4, 1)$

   (i) Calculate distance $|pr|$.

   (ii) Plot points *r*, *p* and *w*.

   (iii) Prove that the area of $\triangle prw$ is equal to 14.

(c) Find *t* given that (2, 3*t*) is on the line $5x + 2y - 4 = 0$.

Question 3

(a) Given $T: 3x - 2y - 12 = 0$

Find:

  (i) Point k, where line T intersects the x-axis.

  (ii) Point l, where line T cuts the y-axis.

  (iii) Calculate the area of the triangle klo where o is the origin.

(b) With $v(3, -4)$ and $w(-2, 6)$ find:

  (i) The slope of $[vw]$.

  (ii) The equation of $[vw]$.

Solution to question 1

(a)

> **(i)** $a(-1, 4)$, $b(5, -10)$. Find point d, the midpoint of $[ab]$.

Midpoint $\left(\dfrac{x_1 + x_2}{2}, \dfrac{y_1 + y_2}{2} \right)$

$a(-1, 4)$ $\qquad\qquad$ $b(5, -10)$

$x_1\, y_1$ $\qquad\qquad$ $x_2\, y_2$

Midpoint $= \left(\dfrac{-1 + 5}{2}, \dfrac{4 - 10}{2} \right)$

$\qquad = \left(\dfrac{4}{2}, \dfrac{-6}{2} \right) = (2, -3)$

$\Rightarrow \qquad\qquad \underline{d(2, -3)}$

> **(ii)** Prove $|ad| = |bd|$.

Evaluate $|ad|$

Distance $= \sqrt{(x_2 - x_1)^2 + (y_2 - y_1)^2}$

$a(-1, 4) \qquad\quad d(2, -3)$

$x_1\, y_1 \qquad\qquad x_2\, y_2$

$= \sqrt{(2 - -1)^2 + (-3 - 4)^2}$

$= \sqrt{(2 + 1)^2 + (-3 - 4)^2}$

$= \sqrt{(3)^2 + (-7)^2}$

$= \sqrt{9 + 49} \quad = \sqrt{58}$

Evaluate $|bd|$

Distance $= \sqrt{(x_2 - x_1)^2 + (y_2 - y_1)^2}$

$b(5, -10) \qquad\qquad d(2, -3)$

$x_1 y_1 \qquad\qquad\qquad x_2 y_2$

$= \sqrt{(2 - 5)^2 + (-3 - -10)^2}$

$= \sqrt{(2 - 5)^2 + (-3 + 10)^2}$

$= \sqrt{(-3)^2 + (7)^2}$

$= \sqrt{9 + 49} = \underline{\sqrt{58}}$

$\Rightarrow \quad |ad| = |bd|$

(b)

$\qquad P: 2x - 6y - 18 = 0$

> **(i)** Find pt. f where line P cuts the x-axis.

'cuts the x-axis' $\rightarrow$ let $y = 0$

$\qquad\qquad 2x - 6y - 18 = 0$

$y = 0$

$\Rightarrow \qquad 2x - 6(0) - 18 = 0$

$\qquad\qquad 2x - 0 - 18 = 0 \quad \Rightarrow \quad 2x = 18$

$\Rightarrow \qquad x = 9$

So, $x = 9$ and $y = 0 \quad \Rightarrow \quad \underline{f(9, 0)}$

> **(ii)** Find pt. g where line P cuts the y-axis.

'cuts the y axis' $\rightarrow$ let $x = 0$

$\qquad\qquad 2x - 6y - 18 = 0$

$x = 0$

$$\Rightarrow \quad 2(0) - 6y - 18 = 0$$

$$0 - 6y - 18 = 0 \quad \Rightarrow \quad -6y = 18$$

$$y = \frac{18}{-6} \quad \Rightarrow y = -3$$

So, $x = 0$ and $y = -3$

$$\Rightarrow \qquad \underline{g(0, -3)}$$

(iii) Find the slope of [fg].

$$\text{Slope} = \frac{y_2 - y_1}{x_2 - x_1}$$

$f(9, 0)$ $\qquad\qquad$ $g(0, -3)$
$x_1\,y_1$ $\qquad\qquad\qquad$ $x_2\,y_2$

$$\text{Slope} = \frac{-3 - 0}{0 - 9} = \frac{-3}{-9}$$

$$= \boxed{+\frac{1}{3}}$$

(iv) Find the equation of [fg].

Again, to find the equation of a line we need:

① The slope of the line (m).

② A point on the line $(x_1\,y_1)$. (We can use either point f or point g.)

Eqn. of [fg]

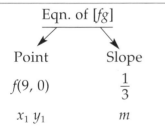

Point $\qquad$ Slope

$f(9, 0)$ $\qquad\qquad \frac{1}{3}$

$x_1\,y_1$ $\qquad\qquad m$

Equation of a line $y - y_1 = m(x - x_1)$

$$\Rightarrow \qquad y - 0 = \frac{1}{3}(x - 9)$$

Bring the bottom part of the fraction across to the left. Do not change sign.

$$\Rightarrow \quad 3(y - 0) = 1(x - 9)$$

$$3y - 0 = 1x - 9$$

Rearrange in the form

| x term | | y term | | number | | = 0 |

$$-1x + 3y + 9 = 0$$

Changing all the signs (to make the x term positive).

$$\underline{1x - 3y - 9 = 0}$$

Solution to question 2

(a)

Given $t(-2, 3)$ and $u(5, -1)$

(i) Find the slope of [tu].

$$\text{Slope} = \frac{y_2 - y_1}{x_2 - x_1}$$

$t(-2, 3)$ $\qquad\qquad u(5, -1)$
$x_1\,y_1$ $\qquad\qquad\quad x_2\,y_2$

$$\text{Slope} = \frac{-1 - 3}{5 - -2} = \frac{-1 - 3}{5 + 2}$$

$$= \boxed{\frac{-4}{7}}$$

(ii) Find the equation of [tu].

Eqn. of [tu]

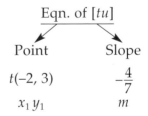

Point $\qquad$ Slope

$t(-2, 3)$ $\qquad\qquad -\frac{4}{7}$

$x_1\,y_1$ $\qquad\qquad\quad m$

Equation of a line $y - y_1 = m(x - x_1)$

$$\Rightarrow \qquad y - 3 = -\frac{4}{7}(x - -2)$$

$$y - 3 = -\frac{4}{7}(x + 2)$$

$$7(y - 3) = -4(x + 2)$$
$$7y - 21 = -4x - 8$$

Rearranging correctly . . .

$$4x + 7y - 21 + 8 = 0$$
$$\underline{4x + 7y - 13 = 0}$$

(b)

$$r(0, -4)\ p(0, 3) \text{ and } w(4, 1)$$

> **(i)   Calculate distance $|pr|$.**

$$\text{Distance} = \sqrt{(x_2 - x_1)^2 + (y_2 - y_1)^2}$$

$$\begin{array}{cc} p(0, 3) & r(0, -4) \\ x_1\,y_1 & x_2\,y_2 \end{array}$$

$$= \sqrt{(0 - 0)^2 + (-4 - 3)^2}$$

$$= \sqrt{(0)^2 + (-7)^2} = \sqrt{49}$$

$$= 7$$

> **(ii)   Plot $r(0, -4)$, $p(0, 3)$ and $w(4, 1)$.**

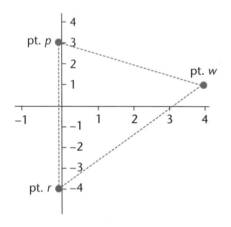

> **(iii) Prove that the area of $\triangle prw$ is 14.**

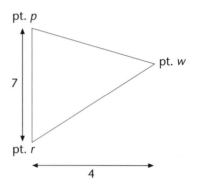

Area of a triangle $= \dfrac{1}{2}$ (base) $\times$ perpendicular height

$$= \dfrac{1}{2}(7) \times (4)$$

$$\Rightarrow \quad \underline{\text{Area } \triangle prw = 14}$$

(c) | **(2, 3t) is on the line**
| **$5x + 2y - 4 = 0$**

$$5x + 2y - 4 = 0$$

Fill in (2, 3t)

$$5(2) + 2(3t) - 4 = 0$$
$$10 + 6t - 4 = 0$$
$$6t + 6 = 0$$
$$6t = -6$$
$$\underline{t = -1}$$

Solution to question 3

(a) $T: 3x - 2y - 12 = 0$

> **(i) Find point k where T cuts the x-axis.**

$$3x - 2y - 12 = 0$$

y = 0

$$\Rightarrow \qquad 3x - 2(0) - 12 = 0$$
$$3x - 0 - 12 = 0$$
$$3x = 12 \quad \Rightarrow \quad x = 4$$

So $x = 4$ and $y = 0$

$\Rightarrow$ $k(4, 0)$

$$3x - 2y - 12 = 0$$

$x = 0$

$\Rightarrow$ $3(0) - 2y - 12 = 0$

$0 - 2y - 12 = 0$

$\Rightarrow$ $-2y = 12 \Rightarrow y = {}^{12}/_{-2}$

$\Rightarrow$ $y = -6$

So, $x = 0$ and $y = -6$

$\Rightarrow$ $\underline{l(0, -6)}$

(iii) Find the area of $\triangle klo$ where 0 is the origin.

Again, the 'origin' is the point $(0, 0)$.

Plot the triangle klo.

$k(4, 0)$ $l(0, -6)$

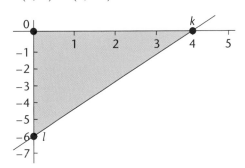

Area = $\frac{1}{2}$ (base) × (perpendicular height)

$\Rightarrow$ Area = $\frac{1}{2}$ (4) × (6)

= $\underline{12}$

(b) Given $v(3, -4)$ and $w(-2, 6)$.

(i) Find the slope of $[vw]$.

$$\text{Slope} = \frac{y_2 - y_1}{x_2 - x_1}$$

$v(3, -4)$ $w(-2, 6)$

$x_1\, y_1$ $x_2\, y_2$

$$\text{Slope} = \frac{6 - -4}{-2 - 3} = \frac{6 + 4}{-2 - 3}$$

$$= \frac{10}{-5} = \boxed{-2}$$

(ii) Find the equation of $[vw]$.

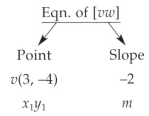

Eqn. of $[vw]$

Point   Slope

$v(3, -4)$ -2

$x_1 y_1$ m

Equation of a line $y - y_1 = m\,(x - x_1)$.

$\Rightarrow$ $y - -4 = -2(x - 3)$

$y + 4 = -2(x - 3)$

$\Rightarrow$ $y + 4 = -2x + 6$

Rearrange . . . $2x + y + 4 - 6 = 0$

$\Rightarrow$ $\underline{2x + y - 2 = 0}$

Chapter **13**
Trigonometry

Section A
Sin, Cos and Tan

Note 1

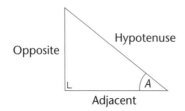

In all right-angled triangles:

① <u>Hypotenuse</u> – opposite the 90° angle.

② <u>Opposite</u> – opposite the second given angle.

③ <u>Adjacent</u> – the side which joins the two angles.

Note 2

Always remember the saying:

'**S**illy **O**ld **H**arry, **C**aught **A** **H**erring, **T**rawling **O**ff **A**merica'

$$\text{Sin} = \frac{\text{Opposite}}{\text{Hypotenuse}}$$

$$\text{Cos} = \frac{\text{Adjacent}}{\text{Hypotenuse}}$$

$$\text{Tan} = \frac{\text{Opposite}}{\text{Adjacent}}$$

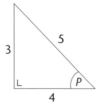

Hypot. = 5   Hypot. = 10

Opp. = 3   Opp. = 8

Adj. = 4   Adj. = 6

$$\text{Sin } P = \frac{\text{Opp.}}{\text{Hypot.}} \qquad \text{Sin } R = \frac{\text{Opp.}}{\text{Hypot.}}$$

$$= \frac{3}{5} \qquad\qquad = \frac{8}{10}$$

$$\text{Cos } P = \frac{\text{Adj.}}{\text{Hypot.}} \qquad \text{Cos } R = \frac{\text{Adj.}}{\text{Hypot.}}$$

$$= \frac{4}{5} \qquad\qquad = \frac{6}{10}$$

$$\text{Tan } P = \frac{\text{Opp.}}{\text{Adj.}} \qquad \text{Tan } R = \frac{\text{Opp.}}{\text{Adj.}}$$

$$= \frac{3}{4} \qquad\qquad = \frac{8}{6}$$

Note 3

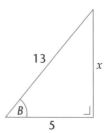

By evaluating x, find:

(i) Tan B.

(ii) Sin B.

In the given diagram:

① We have two sides of a right-angled triangle.

② We are looking for the measure of the third side.

We therefore use the Theory of Pythagoras.

$$\boxed{\text{Hypotenuse}}^2 = \boxed{\text{side 1}}^2 + \boxed{\text{side 2}}^2$$

In the diagram, 13 is the hypotenuse.

$\Rightarrow$ $\qquad 13^2 = 5^2 + x^2$

$\qquad\qquad 169 = 25 + x^2$

$\qquad 169 - 25 = x^2$

$\qquad\qquad 144 = x^2$

$\Rightarrow$ $\qquad\qquad \underline{x = 12}$

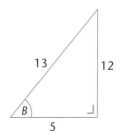

$\Rightarrow$ $\qquad 13 = $ Hypotenuse

$\qquad 12 = $ Opposite

$\qquad 5 = $ Adjacent

(i) $\quad \text{Tan } B = \dfrac{\text{Opp.}}{\text{Adj.}} = \dfrac{12}{5}$

(ii) $\quad \text{Sin } B = \dfrac{\text{Opp.}}{\text{Hypot.}} = \dfrac{12}{13}$

Section B
Using the Calculator

Very important

Before using your calculator ensure that it is in 'DEG' mode (for a 'Sharp' calculator) or in 'D' mode (for a 'Casio' calculator).

This can be seen on the top of the screen.

Type 1

Evaluate Cos 38°11′

'Sharp' calculator

$\boxed{\text{Cos}}$ 38 $\boxed{\text{DMS}}$ 11 $\boxed{\text{DMS}}$ = 0.786 …

'Casio' calculator

$\boxed{\text{Cos}}$ 38 $\boxed{° ′ ″}$ 11 $\boxed{° ′ ″}$ = 0.786 …

Type 2

Evaluate angle A if Tan A = 0.43

'Sharp' calculator

$\boxed{\text{2nd F}}$ $\boxed{\text{Tan}}$ 0.43 = 23.26 …

To express the answer correctly:

$\boxed{\text{2nd F}}$ $\boxed{\text{DMS}}$ $\underline{23°16′}$

'Casio' calculator

$\boxed{\text{Shift}}$ $\boxed{\text{Tan}}$ 0.43 = 23.26 …

$\boxed{\text{Shift}}$ $\boxed{° ′ ″}$ $\underline{23°16′}$

Type 3

Evaluate angle B such that Sin B = $^3/_7$.

'Sharp' calculator

| 2nd F | Sin | 3 | $a^b/_c$ | 7 = 25.37 ...

| 2nd F | DMS | 25°22′

'Casio' calculator

| Shift | Sin | 3 | $a^b/_c$ | 7 = 25.37 ...

| Shift | DMS | 25°22′

Section C
Trigonometric Problem (a)

This is the first of two questions which are asked very frequently.

Please read carefully and follow the steps below when answering any question of this type.

In the diagram
$|ac| = 10$ and $|bc| = 6$

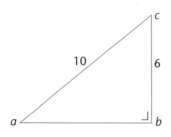

Evaluate:

(i) $|\angle bca|$

(ii) $|\angle bac|$

(i) *Evaluate* $|\angle bca|$.

| Step 1 |

Draw the diag. again, and call what you are looking for x.

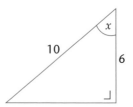

| Step 2 |

Name both sides

10 = Hypotenuse

6 = Adjacent

| Step 3 |

Write out the '9 letters'.

SOH   CAH   TOA

$$\text{Cos} = \frac{\text{Adj.}}{\text{Hypot.}}$$

We chose this because we have the value of both the Adjacent and Hypotenuse.

| Step 4 |

Substitute in the values we have.

$$\text{Cos } x = \frac{6}{10}$$

| Step 5 | *Evaluate x.*

| 2nd F | Cos | 6 | $a^b/_c$ | 10 = 53.13

2nd F   DMS = 53°07'

⇒ |∠bca| = 53°07'

(ii) *Evaluate* |∠bac|.

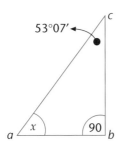

53°07'

c

x   90 b

a

$x + 90° + 53°07' = 180°$

$x + 143°07' = 180°$

$x = 180° - 143°07'$

$x = 36°53'$

⇒ |∠bac| = 36°53'

Section D
Trigonometric Problem (b)

This is the second type of question which is asked very frequently.

The steps are similar to before, so please follow them carefully.

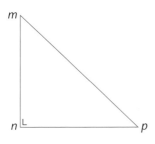

m

n L   p

Given |np| = 7 and |∠mpn| = 42°34', evaluate |mn|.

Evaluate |mn|.

Step 1   *Evaluate* |mn|.

Draw the diagram again and call what we are looking for x.

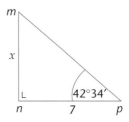

m

x

L   42°34'

n   7   p

Step 2   *Name both sides.*

x = Opposite

7 = Adjacent

Step 3   Write down the '9 letters'.

SOH   CAH   TOA

$$\text{Tan} = \frac{\text{Opp.}}{\text{Adj.}}$$

Step 4   Substitute in the values we have.

$$\text{Tan } 42°34' = \frac{x}{7}$$

Tan 42°34' = 0.9185

⇒ $0.9185 = \frac{x}{7}$

Step 5   Evaluate x.

(Write both sides as a fraction and cross multiply.)

⇒ $\frac{0.9185}{1} = \frac{x}{7}$

⇒ $(0.9185)(7) = (x)(1)$

⇒ $6.43 = x$ ⇒ |mn| = 6.43

135

Section E

Trigonometric Problem (c)

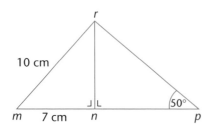

In the given diagram $|mr| = 10$ cm.

$|mn| = 7$ cm and $|\angle npr| = 50°$.

Evaluate ① $|mrn|$

② $|rn|$

③ $|np|$

The steps in Section C and Section D are followed here.

Please be certain about these.

(i) *Evaluate* $|\angle mrn|$.

Draw the left-hand triangle on its own.

①
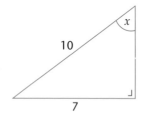

② 10 = Hypotenuse

7 = Opposite

③ SOH   CAH   TOA

⇓

$\text{Sin} = \dfrac{\text{Opp.}}{\text{Hypot.}}$

④ Sin $x = \dfrac{7}{10}$

⑤ 2nd F | Sin (7 $a^b/_c$ 10) = 44.427

2nd F | DMS | 44°25′

⇒ $|\angle mrn| = 44°25′$

(ii) *Evaluate* $|rn|$.

- $\triangle mnr$ is right-angled.
- We know the measure of two of its sides so we can find the third side ($|rn|$) by using the 'Theory of Pythogoras'.

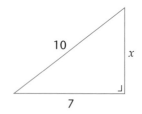

$$10^2 = 7^2 + x^2$$
$$100 = 49 + x^2$$
$$100 - 49 = x^2$$
$$51 = x^2$$
$$\sqrt{51} = x$$

⇒ $\quad 7.1 = x$

So, $|rn| = 7.1$

(iii) *Evaluate* $|np|$.

Draw the right-hand triangle on its own.

①
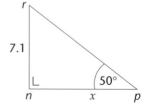

② 7.1 = Opposite

x = Adjacent

③   SOH   CAH   TOA

$$\text{Tan} = \frac{\text{Opp.}}{\text{Adj.}}$$

④ $\text{Tan } 50° = \dfrac{7.1}{x}$

⑤ $\dfrac{1.19}{1} = \dfrac{7.1}{x}$

$(1.19)(x) = 7.1$

$x = \dfrac{7.1}{1.19}$

$x = 5.97$

So, $|np| = 5.97$

Chapter 13
Sample questions for you to try

Question 1

(a)

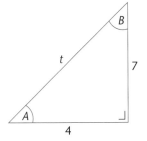

(i)   Evaluate t.

(ii) Express as fractions:

    (a)   Cos A.

    (b)   Sin A.

    (c)   Tan B.

    (d)   Cos B.

(b)

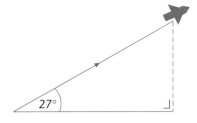

(i)   A plane leaves the ground at a speed of 25 m/sec. How far had it travelled after 3 minutes?

(ii) If the flight path of the plane made a 27° angle with the runway, calculate (to the nearest m) how far above the ground the plane was after 3 minutes.

Question 2

(a)   Sin C = 0.23. Evaluate:

    (i)   Angle C.

    (ii)   Cos C.

    (iii) Tan $2C$.

    (iv) 2 Tan C.

(b)   A flagpole is held up by two ropes such that $|bc|$ = 8 m and $|ab|$ = 7 m.

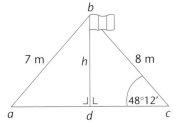

(i)   Calculate the height, h, of the flagpole to the nearest m.

(ii) Calculate $|\angle dab|$.

(iii) Calculate $|\angle dba|$.

Question 3

(a)

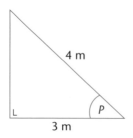

4 m

L

3 m

P

A ladder is shown here leaning against a wall. The bottom of the ladder is 3 m out from the wall.

If the ladder is 4 m in length, calculate p, the angle formed by the ladder and the ground.

(b) If $D = 50°$ and $E = 20°$ Investigate whether the following statements are true or false:

(i) $3 \cos D = \cos 3D$

(ii) $\sin (D + E) = \sin D + \sin E$

(iii) $\tan (D - E) = \tan D - \tan E$

Solution to question 1

(a) (i) Evaluate t.

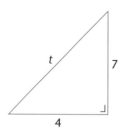

t

7

4

t is the hypotenuse

$$\boxed{\text{Hypotenuse}}^2 = \boxed{\text{side 1}}^2 + \boxed{\text{side 2}}^2$$

$\Rightarrow \quad t^2 = 4^2 + 7^2$

$\quad t^2 = 16 + 49$

$\quad t^2 = 65 \quad \Rightarrow \quad \underline{t = \sqrt{65}}$

(ii)

(a) (b) Evaluate Cos A and Sin A.

$\sqrt{65}$ = Hypotenuse

4 = Adjacent

7 = Opposite

$\sqrt{65}$

7

A

4

$\cos A = \dfrac{\text{Adj.}}{\text{Hypot.}} = \left(\dfrac{4}{\sqrt{65}}\right)$

$\sin A = \dfrac{\text{Opp.}}{\text{Hypot.}} = \left(\dfrac{7}{\sqrt{65}}\right)$

(c) (d) Evaluate Tan B and Cos B.

4 = Opposite

$\sqrt{65}$ = Hypotenuse

7 = Adjacent

B

$\sqrt{65}$

7

4

$\tan B = \dfrac{\text{Opp.}}{\text{Adj.}} = \left(\dfrac{4}{7}\right)$

$\cos B = \dfrac{\text{Adj.}}{\text{Hypot.}} = \left(\dfrac{7}{\sqrt{65}}\right)$

(b)

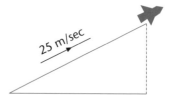

25 m/sec

(i) How far had it travelled after 3 minutes?

3 minutes = 180 seconds

$\Rightarrow$ It travelled (25×180) m

$= \underline{4500 \text{ m}}$

(ii) Calculate the height of the plane above the ground.

Step 1 Mark what we are looking for into the diagram.

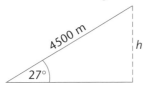

Step 2 Name both sides.

h = Opposite

4500 = Hypotenuse

Step 3 Write out the '9 letters'.

SOH   CAH   TOA

⇓

$$\text{Sin} = \frac{\text{Opp.}}{\text{Hypot.}}$$

Step 4 Fill in the information that we have.

$$\text{Sin } 27° = \frac{h}{4500}$$

Step 5 Evaluate h.

$$\text{Sin } 27° = \frac{h}{4500}$$

$$\boxed{\text{Sin } 27° = 0.454}$$

⇒ $$0.454 = \frac{h}{4500}$$

Again, write both sides in fraction form and cross-multiply.

$$\frac{0.454}{1} = \frac{h}{4500}$$

⇒ $$(0.454)(4500) = (h)(1)$$

$$2042.95 = h$$

So, the plane was 2043 m (to the nearest m) above the ground.

Solution to question 2

(a) Sin C = 0.23

Evaluate:

    (i) **Angle C**

        $C = \underline{13°17'}$

    (ii) **Cos C**

        Cos 13°17' = $\underline{0.9732}$

    (iii) **Tan $2C$**

        = Tan 2(13°17')

        = Tan 26°34'

        = $\underline{0.5}$

    (iv) **2 Tan C**

        = 2(Tan 13°17')

        = 2(0.236)

        = $\underline{0.472}$

(b)

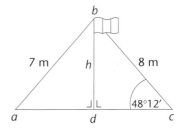

(i) Calculate h, the height of the flagpole.

Step 1

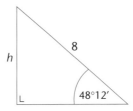

Step 2 h = Opposite

        8 = Hypotenuse

139

| Step 3 | SOH̲ CAH TOA |

$$\text{Sin} = \frac{\text{Opp.}}{\text{Hypot.}}$$

| Step 4 | $\text{Sin } 48°12' = \dfrac{h}{8}$ |

$$\Rightarrow \qquad 0.745 = \frac{h}{8}$$

| Step 5 | $\dfrac{0.745}{1} = \dfrac{h}{8}$ |

$$(0.745)(8) = (h)(1)$$
$$5.96 = h$$

$\Rightarrow$ The height of the flagpole (to the nearest m) is 6 m.

| (ii) Evaluate $|\angle dab|$. |

| Step 1 |

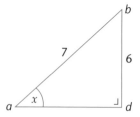

| Step 2 | 6 = Opposite |
| | 7 = Hypotenuse |

| Step 3 | SOH̲ CAH TOA |

$$\text{Sin} = \frac{\text{Opp.}}{\text{Hypot.}}$$

| Step 4 | $\text{Sin } x = \dfrac{6}{7}$ |

| Step 5 | $x = 58°59'$ |

$\Rightarrow \qquad \underline{|\angle dab| = 58°59'}$

| (iii) Evaluate $|\angle dba|$. |

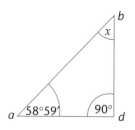

$$58°59' + 90° + x = 180°$$
$$148°59' + x = 180°$$
$$x = 180° - 148°59'$$
$$x = 31°01'$$
$\Rightarrow \qquad |\angle dba| = 31°01'$

Solution to question 3

Calculate p.

| (a) | Step 1 |

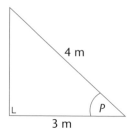

| Step 2 | 3 = Adjacent |
| | 4 = Hypotenuse |

| Step 3 | SOH CA̲H TOA |

$$\text{Cos} = \frac{\text{Adj.}}{\text{Hypot.}}$$

| Step 4 | $\text{Cos } p = \dfrac{3}{4}$ |

| Step 5 | $p = 41°24'$ |
| | $\underline{p = 41°24'}$ |

(b) $D = 50°$ $E = 20°$

Are the following true or false?

(i) 3 Cos D = Cos 3D

Is   3 Cos 50° = Cos 3 (50°)

Is   3 (0.6428) = Cos 150°

                 1.93 ≠ −0.866

⇒   '3 Cos D = Cos 3D' is false

(ii) Sin (D + E) = Sin D + Sin E

Is Sin (50° + 20°) = Sin 50° + Sin 20°

Is   Sin 70° = Sin 50° + Sin 20°

Is   0.94 = 0.766 + 0.342

                 0.94 ≠ 1.108

⇒   'Sin (D + E) = Sin D + Sin E' is false

(iii) Tan (D − E) = Tan D − Tan E

Is Tan (50° − 20°) = Tan 50° − Tan 20°

Is   Tan 30° = Tan 50° − Tan 20°

Is   0.577 = 1.19 − 0.364

                 0.577 ≠ 0.826

⇒   'Tan (D − E) = Tan D − Tan E' is false

Chapter **14**

Sample Paper Two (with detailed solutions)

Question 1

(a)

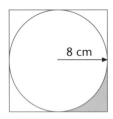

The diagram shows a circle of radius 8 cm inscribed in a square. Calculate:

    (i) The area of the circle. Let π = 3.

    (ii) The area of the square.

    (iii) The area of the shaded area.

(b) (i) A sphere has a curved surface area of 314.16 cm². Calculate the radius of the sphere. Let π = 3.14.

    (ii) Hence evaluate the volume of the sphere in terms of π.

Question 2

(a)

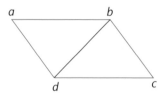

Investigate whether $\triangle abd$ and $\triangle bcd$ are congruent.

(b)

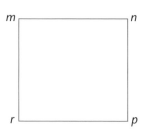

Construct the image of the rectangle under the translation

$$\overrightarrow{mr}$$

(c) Evaluate f and g.

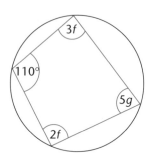

Question 3

(a) In a class of 12, the favourite colours are shown in the pie chart.

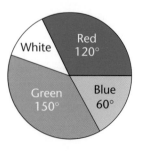

Calculate the number who preferred each colour.

(b) The age of 3 teenagers are as follows:

15 years 8 months

14 years 4 months

17 years 6 months

Calculate their mean age.

Question 4

(a)

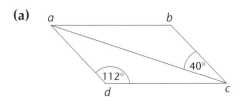

The diagram shows the parallelogram *abcd* with $|\angle adc| = 112°$ and $|\angle bca| = 40°$.

Calculate all other angles.

(b)

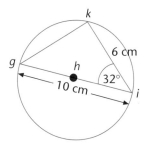

In the diagram *h* is the centre of the circle.

Given $|gi| = 10$ cm, $|ki| = 6$ cm and $|\angle gik| = 32°$ find:

  (i) $|gk|$

  (ii) Area $\triangle gki$

  (iii) $|\angle kgi|$

(c) Construct $\triangle abc$ such that $|ab| = 7$ cm, $|\angle cba| = 70°$ and $|bc| = 8$ cm.

Question 5

(a) Given $L: x - 3y + 6 = 0$

  (i) Find point *a*, where *L* intersects the *x*-axis.

  (ii) Find point *b*, where line *L* cuts the *y*-axis.

  (iii) Find point *c*, the midpoint of [*ab*].

  (iv) Calculate the distance $|ac|$.

  (v) Find the slope of [*bc*].

  (vi) Find the equation of [*bc*].

  (vii) Prove $(3, 3) \in$ line *L*.

Question 6

(a)

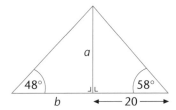

In the diagram above, evaluate *a* and *b*, correct to the nearest whole number.

(b)

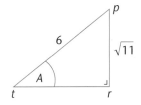

In the given diagram:

  (i) Evaluate $|tr|$.

  (ii) Express Cos *A* as a fraction.

  (iii) Evaluate $|\angle rpt|$.

Solutions to Sample Paper Two

Solution to question 1

(a)

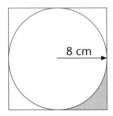

8 cm

    (i)   **Area of circle** $= \pi r^2$

$$= 3 \times 8 \times 8$$

$$= 192 \ cm^2$$

    (ii) **Area of the square** $= l \times w$

$$= 16 \times 16$$

$$= 256 \ cm^2$$

   (iii) **Difference in areas**

$$= 256 \ cm^2 - 192 \ cm^2$$

$$= 65 \ cm^2$$

$\Rightarrow$ **Shaded area** $= 64 \ cm^2 \div 4$

$$= 16 \ cm^2$$

(b) **(i)**

Curved surface area of sphere = 314.16 cm².

$\Rightarrow$ $4\pi r^2 = 314.16$

$\Rightarrow$ $4 \times 3.14 \times r^2 = 314.16$

       $r^2 = 314.16 \div 4 \div 3.14$

       $r^2 = 25$

       $r = \sqrt{25}$

       $r = 5$

So, the radius is 5 cm.

    (ii) Volume of sphere $= \frac{4}{3} \pi r^3$

$$= \frac{4}{3} \times \pi \times 5 \times 5 \times 5$$

$$= \underline{166.67\pi}$$

Solution to question 2

(a)

> **Investigate whether n*abc* and n*bcd* are congruent.**

①   *Are any angles equal?*

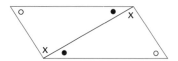

$(\circ) = (\circ)$ …opposite angles in a parallelogram

$(\times) = (\times)$ … alternate angles

$(\bullet) = (\bullet)$ … alternate angles

②   *Are any sides equal?*

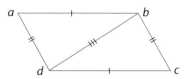

$|ad| = |bc|$ … opposite sides in a parallelogram

$|ab| = |cd|$ … opposite sides in a parallelogram

$|bd| = |bd|$ … same line

③   *Are the triangles congruent?*

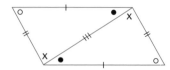

Therefore the triangles <u>are</u> congruent because of *SAS* (or *AAS*, *SSS* or *RHS*).

(b)

Construct the image of the rectangle under the translation $\overrightarrow{mr}$.

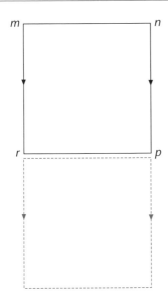

(c) Evaluate f and g.

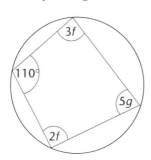

$3f + 2f = 180°$	$110° + 5g = 180°$
$\Rightarrow \quad 5f = 180°$	$5g = 180° - 110°$
$\Rightarrow \quad f = \dfrac{180°}{5}$	$5g = 70°$
$\underline{f = 36°}$	$\Rightarrow \quad g = \dfrac{70°}{5}$
	$\underline{g = 14°}$

Solution to question 3

(a)

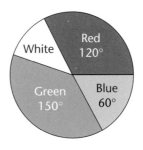

The favourite colour of 12 pupils is represented in the pie chart. Calculate the number who prefer each colour.

Red

$$\frac{\text{Angle representing red}}{\text{Total angle}} \times \frac{12}{1} \text{ (total}$$

number)

$$= \frac{120°}{360°} \times \frac{12}{1} = 4 \text{ people}$$

Blue

$$= \frac{60°}{360°} \times \frac{12}{1} = 2 \text{ people}$$

Green

$$\frac{150°}{360°} \times \frac{12}{1} = 5 \text{ people}$$

White

Angle representing white

$$= 360° - (120° + 60° + 150°)$$
$$= 360° - 330° = 30°$$
$$\Rightarrow \quad \frac{30°}{360°} \times \frac{12}{1} = 1 \text{ person}$$

Check

4 people + 2 people + 5 people + 1 person = 12 people ✓

(b) The ages of three people are:

15 years 8 months

14 years 4 months

17 years 6 months

Calculate the mean age.

To find the mean age, we add the ages and divide by 3.

$$\begin{array}{r} 15 \text{ years} \quad 8 \text{ months} \\ 14 \text{ years} \quad 4 \text{ months} \\ + \ 17 \text{ years} \quad 6 \text{ months} \\ \hline 46 \text{ years} \ 18 \text{ months} \end{array}$$

Convert to months.

$$46 \text{ years} = (46 \times 12) \text{ months}$$
$$= 552 \text{ months}$$

$\Rightarrow$ 46 years 18 months = *570 months*

Divide by 3.

$$570 \text{ months} \div 3 = 190 \text{ months}$$

Convert to years and months.

12$\big|$19^{7}0

15 rem. 10 = 15 years 10 months

Solution to question 4

(a)

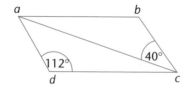

Calculate all angles.

146

(x) = (x) … alternate angles

(∘) = (∘) … alternate angles

(•) = (•) … opposite angles in a parallelogram

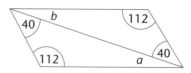

① $40° + 112° + a = 180°$

$152° + a = 180°$

$a = 180° - 152°$

$\Rightarrow$ $\underline{a = 28°}$

② $a = b \Rightarrow \underline{b = 28°}$

(b)

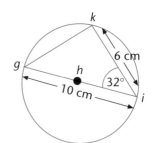

(i) Evaluate $|gk|$ and area Δgki.

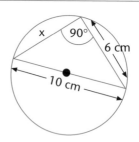

$$10^2 = 6^2 + x^2$$
$$100 = 36 + x^2$$
$$100 - 36 = x^2$$
$\Rightarrow$ $$64 = x^2$$
$$\sqrt{64} = x$$
$\Rightarrow$ $$\underline{|gk| = 8}$$

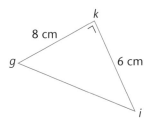

(ii) Area of $\triangle gki = \dfrac{1}{2}$ (base) × (perp. height)

$$= \dfrac{1}{2}(8) \times (6) = \underline{24}$$

(iii) Evaluate $|\angle kgi|$.

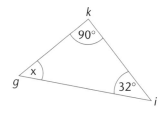

$$x + 90° + 32° = 180°$$
$$x + 122° = 180°$$
$$\Rightarrow \qquad\qquad x = 180° - 122°$$
$$x = 58°$$
$$\Rightarrow \qquad |\angle kgi| = 58°$$

(c)

Construct n*abc* such that
$|ab|$ = 7 cm, $|\angle cba|$ = 70° and
$|bc|$ = 8 cm.

Rough diagram

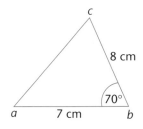

Construct the triangle.

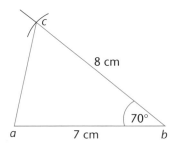

Solution to question 5

(a) Given $L: x - 3y + 6 = 0$

(i) Find point a, where L intersects the x-axis.

$$x - 3y + 6 = 0$$
Let $y = 0$
$$x - 3(0) + 6 = 0$$
$$\Rightarrow \quad x - 0 + 6 = 0 \qquad \Rightarrow \quad x = -6$$
So, $x = -6$ and $y = 0$
$$\Rightarrow \quad \underline{a(-6,\,0)}$$

(ii) Find point b, where L cuts the y-axis.

$$x - 3y + 6 = 0$$
Let $x = 0$
$$0 - 3y + 6 = 0$$
$$\Rightarrow \quad -3y = -6 \quad \Rightarrow y = \dfrac{-6}{-3}$$
$$y = + 2$$
So, $x = 0$ and $y = 2$
$$\Rightarrow \qquad\qquad \underline{b(0,\,2)}$$

(iii) Find point c, the midpoint of $[ab]$.

$$\text{Midpoint} = \left(\dfrac{x_1 + x_2}{2},\, \dfrac{y_1 + y_2}{2} \right)$$

$$a(-6, 0) \qquad\qquad b(0, 2)$$
$$x_1 \, y_1 \qquad\qquad\qquad x_2 \, y_2$$

$$= \left(\frac{-6 + 0}{2}, \frac{0 + 2}{2} \right)$$

$$= \left(\frac{-6}{2}, \frac{2}{2} \right) \;\Rightarrow\; c(-3, 1)$$

(iv) Calculate the distance |ac|.

$$\text{Distance} = \sqrt{(x_2 - x_1)^2 + (y_2 - y_1)^2}$$

$$a(-6, 0) \qquad\qquad c(-3, 1)$$
$$x_1 \, y_1 \qquad\qquad\qquad x_2 \, y_2$$

$$= \sqrt{(-3 - -6)^2 + (1 - 0)^2}$$

$$= \sqrt{(-3 + 6)^2 + (1 - 0)^2}$$

$$= \sqrt{(-3)^2 + (1)^2} \;=\; \sqrt{9 + 1}$$

$$\Rightarrow \;\; |ac| = \sqrt{10}$$

(v) Find the slope of [bc].

$$\text{Slope} = \frac{y_2 - y_1}{x_2 - x_1}$$

$$b(0, 2) \qquad\qquad c(-3, 1)$$
$$x_1 \, y_1 \qquad\qquad\qquad x_2 \, y_2$$

$$= \frac{1 - 2}{-3 - 0} = \frac{-1}{-3} = \frac{1}{3}$$

(vi) Find the equation of [bc].

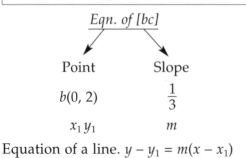

$$\underline{\textit{Eqn. of } [bc]}$$

Point   Slope

$b(0, 2)$ $\dfrac{1}{3}$

$x_1 \, y_1$ m

Equation of a line. $y - y_1 = m(x - x_1)$

$$\Rightarrow \;\; y - 2 = \tfrac{1}{3}(x - 0)$$

$$3(y - 2) = 1(x + 0)$$

$$3y - 6 = 1x$$

Rearrange ... $\underline{1x - 3y + 6 = 0}$

(vii) Prove (3, 3) is on the line
$x - 3y + 6 = 0$.

$$x - 3y + 6 = 0$$

Fill in (3, 3)

$$3 - 3(3) + 6 = 0$$

$$3 - 9 + 6 = 0$$

$$0 = 0 \quad \checkmark$$

As (3, 3) satisfies the equation, the point is on the line.

Solution to question 6

(a)

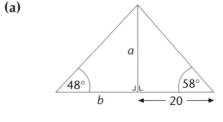

Evaluate a.

Step 1

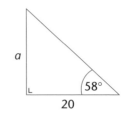

Step 2 a = Opposite
               20 = Adjacent

Step 3 SOH   CAH   TOA
                                 ⇓

$$\text{Tan} = \frac{\text{Opp.}}{\text{Adj.}}$$

148

Step 4	Tan 58° = $\frac{a}{20}$

$\Rightarrow$ $1.6 = \frac{a}{20}$

Step 5	$\frac{1.6}{1} = \frac{a}{20}$

$\Rightarrow$ $(1.6)(20) = (a)(1)$

$$\boxed{a = 32}$$

Evaluate b.

Step 1

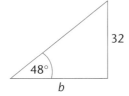

Step 2	b = Adjacent
	32 = Opposite

Step 3	SOH CAH TOA

$$\Downarrow$$

$$\text{Tan} = \frac{\text{Opp.}}{\text{Adj.}}$$

Step 4	Tan 48° = $\frac{32}{b}$

$\Rightarrow$ $1.11 = \frac{32}{b}$

Step 5	$\frac{1.11}{1} = \frac{32}{b}$

$$(1.11)(b) = (1)(32)$$

$\Rightarrow$ $b = \frac{32}{1.11}$

$$b = 28.8$$

So, $b = 29$ correct to the nearest whole number.

(b)

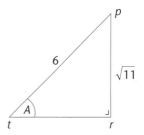

(i) Evaluate $|tr|$.

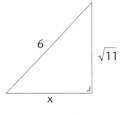

$$6^2 = (\sqrt{11})^2 + x^2$$

$$36 = 11 + x^2$$

$\Rightarrow$ $36 - 11 = x^2$

$$25 = x^2$$

$\Rightarrow$ $\sqrt{25} = x$

So, $\underline{|tr| = 5}$

(ii) Find Cos A.

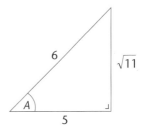

$$6 = \text{Hypot.}$$

$$5 = \text{Adj.}$$

$$\sqrt{11} = \text{Opp.}$$

$$\text{Cos } A = \frac{\text{Adj.}}{\text{Hypot.}} = \left(\frac{5}{6}\right)$$

(iii) Evaluate $|\angle rpt|$.

Step 1

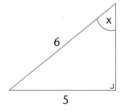

Step 2   6 = Hypotenuse
              5 = Opposite

Step 3   SOH   CAH   TOA
                      ⇓

$$Sin = \frac{Opp.}{Hypot.}$$

Step 4 $Sin\ x = \dfrac{5}{6}$

Step 5 ⇒ $x = 56°26'$

So, $\underline{|\angle rpt| = 56°26'}$

150